**Disclaime**r

This book is designed to provide Basic Information
on Starting an Investment Club.

Serve as an easy to understand, fun and Workable Guide

For those interested in starting a Private Investment Club.

Encouraging, directing and conceiving ideas.

A great source to guide you in your investment endeavors

# "Start A Successful Investment Club to Secure Your Financial Freedom and Retirement."

### It's Time to Maximize Your Investment Potential and Do it NOW

*An easy to understand, fun guide for anyone to start, manage
And profit from an investment club*

## JOHN C. JONES

# "Start A Successful Investment Club to Secure Your Financial Freedom and Retirement."

### It's Time to Maximize Your Investment Potential and Do it NOW

*An easy to understand, fun guide for anyone to start, manage And profit from an investment club*

**PENDIUM PUBLISHING HOUSE**
514-201 DANIELS STREET
RALEIGH, NC 27605

For information, please visit our Web site at
*www.pendiumpublishing.com*

PENDIUM Publishing and its logo
are registered trademarks.

**"Start A Successful Investment Club to Secure Your Financial Freedom and Retirement.**
By John C. Jones

Copyright © John C. Jones, 2019
All Rights Reserved.

ISBN: 978-1-944348-12-0

PUBLISHER'S NOTE

Without limiting the rights under the copyright reserved above, no part of this publication may be reproduced, stored in or introduced into a retrieval system, or transmitted, in any form, or by any means (electronic, mechanical, photocopying, recording, or otherwise), without the prior written permission of both the copyright owner and the above publisher of this book.

If you purchased this book without a cover you should be aware that the book is stolen property. It was reported as "unsold and destroyed" to the publisher and neither the author nor the publisher has received any payment for this "stripped book."

This book is printed on acid-free paper.

**Investment Club** – If you were to go onto the Internet and look at website: http://www.investorwords.com/2608/investment club. html#ixzz590wMazao:

You will find that it is a group of individuals who meet for the purpose of pooling some of their money in small groups and deciding how to invest the money. Like-Minded Investors come together to make investments based upon the input and research of the entire group, often providing a more complete foundation for subsequent decisions. Of course, members of investment clubs do not need to invest only through the club. The club can make an excellent addition to a portfolio or it can serve as an excellent introduction to investing as an individual.

Clubs can be a benefit to investors of all skill and experience levels. It can be difficult to gain a spot in an existing club without connections or the opportunity to replace a departing member. Fortunately, starting a new club is as simple as finding a dozen or so people in one geographic area who want to participate. Members should plan to and will be required to contribute at least a certain amount of money to the club's investment budget at certain intervals. Some clubs allow members to exceed the minimum and others do not. All investments should be researched as carefully as an individual would research them, but because more people are involved, research can be more thorough and cover more investment opportunities.

Members typically meet on a periodic basis to make investment decisions as a group through a voting process and recording of minutes. This group of individuals gather information, collect a specified amount of money from each individual and perform investment transactions outside of the group.

Our club members started out paying $100.00 a month and the amount was increased to $105.00 a month ($5.00 was to cover bank maintenance fees, stamps, envelopes, printers ink, copy paper and a receipt book). The President recommended and the club members agreed that club dues should increase by $5.00 each year. However, once the membership dues reached $110.00 a month, members didn't want to increase it anymore.

An investment club provides an avenue where members of similar interests can learn about investment markets. There is a glossary in the back of the book that explains various investment terminology.

According to the website: https://www.betterinvesting.org, individuals can make money and have fun at the same time. The club members not only enjoy the extra dividends but can watch their portfolio grow. Also, members can take out money for college or take a dream vacation. This website teaches you how to understand stocks so you will have confidence when investing.

An investment club provides the opportunity for members to share the load and pool their knowledge and money to learn more with less time and effort than they can on their own.

Investment Clubs are an excellent way to stay focused, gain experience and accelerate investment learning. Social interaction with like-minded members also adds an important and enjoyable dimension to the club experience. New investors find that a club provides a safe and supportive environment to learn the basics of investing., while experienced investors gain an opportunity to sharpen investing skills. All club members benefit in added buying power through a shared portfolio that enables the club to invest in stocks that an individual may not be able to afford on their own and quickly build a diversified portfolio.

# INTRODUCTION

### The quest to succeed is like a raging fire that won't go out!

First of all, I want to take this time out to thank you for buying my book. I actually finished this book in February of 2001. I know what you're probably wondering, why did it take me so long to publish it and put it on the market? Well, I try to put people first and not just think of how much money I could make from the sale of this book. I know for sure now is the right time to put the book on the market.

Just look at the state of the economy: 6.7 Million People are still without a job according to Bureau of Labor Statistics for January 2018. Even in 2018, Education is being put on the Back Burner because Congress is still fighting over government funding and government debt. Find this on https://www.the74million.org to verify this information.

CEO's are giving themselves Million Dollar Raises while employees of the same company are losing their jobs. Here is a prime example: Last April (2010), the Baltimore Sun reported that Stanley Black and Decker in Towson, MD, announced plans to lay off 4,000 of its 38,000 employees.

Yet, according to USA Today, Stanley Black & Decker CEO John Lundgren made more than $32 million in 2010, up 253.1 percent from the previous year.

Congressmen agree to a rate hike in minimum wage but 94% of Congressmen don't pay the hike to their interns, according to a USA Today Report in 2015.

Big Corporations that seemed financially sound in the past are going BELLY UP or filing Bankruptcy. According to www.ReasonPad.com, top ranked companies went bankrupt in 2009 (Lehman Brothers, Washington Mutual, WorldCom, General Motors, Enron, Conesco, Chrysler, Thornburg Mortgage, Pacific Gas and Electric company and Texaco.

You get the picture: we as citizens need to plot out our own destinies. It's time for Families all across the United States and the World to create and maintain a Financial Empire.

Here is what I mean, from the time our children are born, we need to start and maintain an investment towards their financial future. By during this, we can finance our children's education and start them out with a "nest egg towards their futures." Many Families are mortgaging their houses to the hilt and spending all of their retirement savings towards college education.

Somehow, we've gone from being self-reliant families to dependent families! I wrote this book because I want everyone to know that it isn't necessary to have a lot of money to start an investment club. I didn't have a lot of money but I've always felt that you could reach greater heights or invest in the stock market by pooling your resources.

James Stowers, Jr., was an entrepreneur who applied Midwestern values of preparation, integrity and collegiality to the founding of American Century Investments in 1958. He used these same strategies to create The Stowers Institute for Medical Research in 1994, according to https://www.stowers.org. James E. Stowers was ranked among the top ten by Forbes Magazine as one of the most generous people on the planet. Mr. Stowers figured that creating knowledge was the most powerful contribution he could offer mankind.

In 1992, James Stowers wrote a book entitled, "Yes You Can Achieve Financial Independence." He was a great inspiration to me in trying to write this book. He says, "You shouldn't look at your present condition and figure that's your destiny but you should look at your life as to what it can be."

If you've always felt like you wanted to be in the stock market but couldn't, you should seriously think about an investment club. Whether you're young or old, you can benefit from an investment club. If you can't find one, start your own.

Another quote from James Stowers' book, "I didn't just float through life and let whatever comes my way. I decided to map out my own course in life."

As far back as I can remember, I've always wanted to experience freedom. As a young boy, my brothers and I dug a fishing pond. We went to different places and caught different kinds of fish. It was so exciting putting those fish in our very own pond. We waited a long time for the fish to grow. Finally, we were able to fish in our very own pond; that was one of the greatest feelings I can remember! I didn't realize it at the time, but what I really wanted was the freedom to do what I wanted when I wanted.

I first started learning about investing from Charles J. Givens: I found out from him indirectly because I was reading his book, "Wealth Without Risk." In his book, he mentioned a book by James E. Stowers entitled, "Yes You Can Achieve Financial Independence." This book was about how James Stowers started the investment firm of Twentieth Century Investors (currently, "American Century Investors").

Charjes J. Givens was very inspirational to me in writing this book. He was a bestselling author of two books (Wealth Without Risk and Financial Self Defense). He founded the Charles J. Givens Organization that grew to over 450,000 Members. Charles Givens frequently appeared on nationally syndicated daytime television shows to promote his financial strategies, and hosted a weekly radio program. Information was gathered from https://www.archive.org/details/Financial Library Charles Givens.

The book by James E. Stowers caught my deepest curiosity and I ordered it and waited anxiously for it to arrive. Once the book arrived, I couldn't put it down! I read the book many times from cover to cover. That's how I got into investing. I tried to overdo it when I first started investing. My wife and I had five (5) different accounts (an IRA for me, one for my wife, a joint account, an account for my son and one for my daughter). We kept those accounts for 7 or 8 years. We would save a little and withdraw it almost as fast as we were saving it!

All during this time, I was fertilizing, conceiving and about to give birth to an investment club. I talked to my wife (Angela) about it. The next thing I knew, she had checked out three different types of books from the Knightdale, NC Library on starting an investment club. After devouring the books from cover to cover, I started talking to friends and neighbors and anyone who would listen.

Everything was going well until man's # 1 enemy, fear set in: Fear that no one really understood the dream; fear that no one would be consistent and fear that no one would want to do this. I try to reflect back on the word of GOD when I face something in life that's challenging. I thought about what 2 Timothy 1:7 (NASB) says, and my God hath not given us a spirit of timidity, but of power, and love, and discipline." Also, I thought about what it says in Philippians 4:19 (NASB), and my God will supply all your needs according to his riches in glory in Christ Jesus.

After that, I mentioned it to my wife (Angela), and she said, "If you're serious, you need to pray about it and move forward with it" So, I talked to a group of Army Buddies I knew and told them I was going to start an investment club. Three or four months passed and I hadn't done anything. One of the soldiers I had talked to asked, "Are you going to start this investment club or not?" So, on February 20, 1999, I started the "Financial Freedom (-FINFREE-) Investment Club."

At our first meeting, seven people attended and all seven people joined.! The membership got up to twelve and now, we're going into our 20th. year and have seven committed members. We started out paying $105.00 a month ($100.00 to invest and $5.00 for an administrative fee); The administrative fee was for bank service charges. We finally found a bank with free checking (administrative fee is no longer required of members).

This is a fun, easy to understand book for anyone who desires to earn Maximum Profit on Investments, and desires clear and easy-to-understand information on group investing. Also, if you desire to achieve financial security, realize there is potential for greater profit through group investing. Lastly, this book will increase your readiness for retirement at any age, address the enemy (fear) and include sample forms and charts to aid you in setting up a profitable investment club.

# ACKNOWLEDGEMENTS

From the bottom of my heart, I'd like to thank a few people who encouraged me when I was trying to Write This Book:

To GOD, for giving me the Inspiration to write a step by step Guide to help Every Day People, like myself, who want to venture into the Stock Market.

To my wife, Angela, who checked out the books from the Knightdale, NC Library for me when she knew I was interested in starting an Investment Club. Anything that I've ever had an interest in, Angela has Always been very encouraging to me and very supportive of me.

To my daughter, Mallory and my son, Jermondo, who Think I'm the greatest dad in the whole wide world! They Always tell me, "daddy", you can do it!"

To my Investment Club Members, who were Really Excited

When I first started talking about starting an investment club.

I was very excited when seven people showed up for my first meeting and all seven joined.

To my Mother (Liza) and Father (Cleveland), who helped me keep my Spiritual Life in order.

To Matthew Battle because he and I have been friends for a long time. He has always been very encouraging, even when my ideas didn't make sense.

To Melvin Fox who has been very dedicated, devoted and a good friend. I remember when I would hold meetings and Melvin and I were the only ones present.

To CSM Ly, who is a club member and a very good friend of mine.

# FOREWORD

**By: CSM Randy Ly**

We have been friends for more than fifteen years and have watched one another grow and we have learned an immense amount from one another. We have talked about everything from family, goals, business, and even the investment club. Mr. Jones talked to me several times over the years about his aspirations to finish the book he was writing and promised that he would one day complete it; however, he never discussed what it was about with me during the first few years. He was extremely selective about sharing information and welcoming new members into his investment club.

As you will read later, in this very book, that is exactly how it is supposed to work. Everyone should not be afforded the opportunity to join your investment club. Everyone does not deserve to benefit from the successes or learning experiences associated with being a member of an investment club. Investment Clubs are not for the faint of heart, someone who is looking to gain millions overnight, or a short term investment opportunity. They are for members who know the benefits of gains in masses, forming friendships and caring for one another.

Mr. Jones invited me to join the club several years after we initially met and I felt honored with just the offer. I know without a shadow of a doubt that I had nothing to worry about as long as I was doing business with him. We have now been contributing for quite a few years and I have enjoyed the camaraderie with him and his family. It feels great to know that we continue to teach, learn and ultimately benefit from one another, but are growing as friends and families.

Mr. Jones has spent countless hours researching all of the information and he laid it out here in an extremely simple fashion and quick read to benefit all of you. He himself took the reins after all of this research and stepped out on a limb, knowing and trusting in his faith that he would succeed and be able to share his experiences and knowledge with all who digest this book. I know that without any other means someone can take this book and put it to use and they too can say that Mr. Jones is a very intelligent, considerate and wonderful person. He is a great father, husband, Christian, friend, leader, mentor, co-worker, confidant, and professional. My first interaction with him was over the phone in 2003, dealing with a work event. He was very considerate and understanding about my situation and assisted me in fixing the dilemma immediately without even meeting me.

I gained a lot of respect for him in that moment and later had the opportunity to meet and work with him directly. Mr. Jones and I seemed to hit it off immediately and our friendship grew through mutual respect, work relations and personal interactions. He is one of the most honest and trustworthy people that I have ever met. Mr. Jones is the type of individual who can get along with virtually anyone and will go out of his way to ensure that they know someone cares about them. He makes it a point to try his best to wish them a good day or just say something encouraging to them. He believes in helping people and does just that through many different methods and running an effective investment club.

How do I know this, you ask? Well, the answer is very simple, this man has the experience, has tried and tested all of what he laid out here for you. He is cutting straight to the chase and wants nothing more than to see you "finish YOUR race to financial freedom." This book is another great example of Mr. Jones' mission in life to help people be better and do better.

# Starting the Investment Club

This book will get you set up and running without any problems. I can't tell you which stocks, bonds or Mutual Funds to pick. I can't say this enough, if your club is thinking seriously about a particular fund to invest in, there is nothing better than doing your homework. What I mean by this is, once you find a fund that the club members are interested in, gather such information like:

> How long has the fund been in existence?
> What kind of interest rate did it pay for the last year, the past three and five years?
> What types of companies are involved in this fund?
> What's the minimum investment?
> Get a prospectus and read about the fund

There are agencies out there that can assist you in your investment endeavors. One is the National Association of Investors Corporation (NAIC). This organization was founded in 1951 and is headquartered in Madison Heights, Michigan. It states as it's purpose: To teach individuals to become successful Common Stock Investors and build wealth over their lifetimes through management of their own investments. The NAIC also states that they will help you understand the theory of investing, provide information on when to sell, and information on picking good stocks in any market.

There is another agency out there called the American Association of Individual Investors (AAII). This is a non-profit organization founded in 1978 and headquartered in Chicago. The author found out that the organization states its purpose is to assist individuals in becoming effective managers of their own assets through programs of education, information, and research. I'm not saying that these organizations won't help you. My advice to you is, be careful about getting into too much debt when your club first begin. Some of the information will be free but there will be things like monthly subscriptions that will cost you. All I'm trying to say is, get your club established and be careful about your initial debt.

# Contents

1. Becoming Financially Free ............................................. 29

    Forgotten Dreams or A Friend Called Fear? ............................ 29
    What Gets You Excited? ................................................ 32
    Why Some People Never Pursue Their Dreams ....................... 33
    Common Myths That Can Keep Us Poor ................................ 35
    Forty Years and A Gold Watch or You Need to Provide Your
    Own Golden Parachute ................................................ 38
    When to Start Investing ............................................... 40
    Do I Go IT Alone After the Club Is Started? ........................... 43
    Where Do I Get the Money to Invest? ................................... 44
    Saving Is easy, Commitment is hard ................................... 46

2. Start Out The Right Way And Your Club Will Be
   Successful .......................................................... 48

    Recruiting the right club members ..................................... 49
    Financial Freedom ("Finfree") Investment Club Recruiting
    Sheet .................................................................. 52
    You Must Obtain a Tax Identification Number from the IRS 58
    Certificate of Assumed Names form must be obtained
    from the Register of Deeds ............................................ 59
    A Partnership Agreement Must Be Drawn Up Once
    You Get Members To Join Your Club .................................... 60
    Accounting For Monies Donated ........................................ 69

3. Setting Up Your Club To Run Like
   A Well Oiled Machine .................................................... 71

   Sample Monthly Newsletter ......................................... 71
   Financial Freedom ("Finfree") ® Investment Club ®
   Requirements ............................................................... 76
   Operating Procedures And Club Officers ................................. 77
   Set Goals So The Club Members Will Know
   What You're Aiming For ............................................... 79
   Local Bank Account ..................................................... 82
   Which Mutual Fund/Stock Company .......................... 83

4. How To Keep The Club Members Motivated And
   Focused On Club Goals ................................................ 91

   Designated Place And Time For Periodic Meetings ................ 91
   Agenda For Each Time The Club Meets To Conserve Time .. 92
   Guest Speakers Who Will Come And Share Their Success
   Stories ........................................................................... 93
   Special Events Where Family Members Are Invited ............... 94
   Ensure Club Members Get Financial Statements
   On A Regular Basis ...................................................... 96

5. What To Do If A Member Dies Or Becomes
   Incapacitated? ............................................................... 98

6. Find An Organization Who That Will Do
   The Club's Tax Returns .............................................. 100

7. Bibliography ............................................................... 103

8. Basic Investment Terminology .................................. 119

# BECOMING FINANCIALLY FREE

**Forgotten Dreams or A Friend Called Fear?**

When you read my book, you're going to either love me or hate me. But it really doesn't matter which one you decide to do. The important thing is that you act now and don't continue to let time that you've been given on this earth continue to evaporate, ignoring the wisdom of using it wisely.

Allow me now to introduce you to Fear, who over the years has served as both my best friend and worst enemy. There have been times when I was afraid and that fear caused me to be more careful regarding what I was saying or the subject I was speaking on. I would say in this case, I used fear to work for me. Sometimes we can be too confident and this will cause us to be cockey or arrogant. When this happens, things can go wrong or not as planned. If you use fear to stay in your comfort zone or refrain from taking on new challenges, I believe that fear will keep you from moving forward.

Here is one of Marilyn Monroe's famous quotes, "You never know what life is like until you have lived it." Marilyn is saying that unless you get out and live your life, you won't really know what life is like. It's like she's saying some people live and die without knowing what life is like. You have to get out and do the things you want to do, tell people the things you've been wanting to do, tell people the things you've been wanting to say and feel the feelings that come with living a life that is meaningful and interesting. You don't have to live to anyone's standards, as each of us has our own idea of what it means to live life to the fullest. This information was taken from www.brightdrops.com/marilyn-monroe-quotes.

Think about it for a moment - as you were growing up and trying to please people, were they ever satisfied? I know in my life I could never please people. To go a step further, people can't please themselves. we don't go after our dreams because of fear. I want you to do one thing for me right now. Tell fear to pack its suitcase and get out of your life.

When I was a teenager, growing up in a very rural, small town, I decided that I was going to write a novel (a love story). I managed to finish about twenty pages before my parents asked me what I was writing and I said a love story.

They were very "encouraging" when they said, "boy, you know you can't make any money writing books." With those "encouraging words," I threw my papers away and forgot about my novel. I really never thought about it again until I started to write this book.

Then there was the time in Elementary School when I discovered that I could draw fairly well. I continued my artistic efforts through most of high school. There was a time in the tenth grade when all biology students were required to draw a picture of a microscope on a poster board. My detailed, realistic picture was selected as best out of the entire class and was displayed at the school for years after I graduated. I was feeling pretty confident of my artistic ability after this. So, I entered an Art Talent Drawing Contest. My score was 97 out of a possible 100 on the test. After that, I talked to my father about attending art school to become a Commercial Artist. Again, my father was "very encouraging" when he said, "Boy, you can't make any money from drawing. Once again, I quickly abandoned a dream.

Let's go a little further back when I was in the first or second grade. I'm from a large family and my father had me and two of my younger brothers sitting on a bench on our porch. My father had us counting from one to forty. I was sitting in the middle and when my turn came, I made the mistake of saying Twenty - nine, forty.

My father, whose reaction was akin to what is commonly referred to as a "conniption" said, "You might as well quit school now and catch a pulp wood truck to earn your living because you're not learning anything in school." Good grief, I was a child, I made a mistake.

See how "encouraging" parents can be when kids have dreams? I wonder if it's because no one encouraged them to pursue their dreams when they were growing up. I think it's a generational thing and fear is the culprit. We can look at what happened to me in a number of ways, I can blame my parents for my lack of success or I can break that cycle of fear by embracing courage and pursuing my God-given potential.

Which one do you think will work best for me? Well, if I do nothing, I'll be just like the person who wants to win a race but never enters. You know what will happen if you do nothing but by entering the race, you always have a chance.

## What Gets You Excited?

Think about all of the events in life that are thrilling and exciting. These things are only exciting because of an audience. Think about the NASCAR races or the Indianapolis 500 without an audience (no people watching, no sponsors or media coverage). Can you picture it?

Fifty cars going around the racetrack for 500 laps and no one watching and no media coverage. When I look at the situation in these terms, I think of an event that's really boring! Let's look at some other events: Hockey Games with just the hockey players, the NBA with just the players, a preacher in church preaching with no one around. Some things in life are meaningless without an audience. So, what am I getting at? Well, when you find a solid stock or mutual fund, you can invest without an audience. With an investment club, you don't need an audience, just a few people with the same vision, commitment and goals and cruise on towards a secured Financial Retirement.

**Why Some People Never Pursue Their Dreams**

I believe in order for any family, organization, or group to progress and move forward, it must have a vision. There is a famous quote that goes something like this, "Some people say that they have to see it before they can believe it." But the reality is, "You have to believe it before you can see it."

You have to have a clear picture in your mind of what you want in order to accomplish it. In other words, you must have a vision Proverbs 29:18 (KJV) supports the vision statement. It reads like this: Where there is no vision, the people perish. But he that keepeth the law, happy is he.. A vision will cause you to be able to see through the fog and have a clear picture in your mind of what you want to accomplish and believe that you can do it. Philippians 4:13 (NASB) says, "I can do all things through CHRIST which strengthens me." We need to realize that GOD doesn't want us to fail. GOD has created an unlimited potential in us. We have to work and pursue our dreams. I broke the word VISION down and explained it in my own words:

V – Value - it must be so important to you that there is a burning desire to accomplish your goal.

I – Image - You will be able to see it so clearly until it will be as though you were holding a picture before your eyes.

S – Sacred - it must be so valuable to you until you will treasure it to the day of its completion and beyond.

I – Innovative - you must be able to take what you have and update it to make it relevant.

O – Optimistic - you must be excited to the point of having a burning desire to make your idea successful.

N – Needed - you will know that people will be better off and that their lives will be much more profitable and productive by making use of your ideas. Also, you must feel that there is such a need for your ideas until you can't imagine people living without it.

## Common Myths That Can Keep Us Poor

Some people hesitate to move forward in life because they have some wrong ideas or myths about money.

Dave Ramsey is an American Financial author, radio host heard on over 500 radio stations in the United States, television personality and motivational speaker, with a net worth of $55 million dollars. He strongly discourages the use of debt. Below are the twenty-five common myths about money:

**But . . . I Just Can't Save.**

1. I'll save next year when I'm making more money.
2. At my age, it's too late anyway.
3. Why save money? You can't take it with you when you die.

**Cars are the exception.**

4. Old cars just aren't as safe.
5. What's wrong with a 72-month car payment?

6. My car is an investment.
7. Buying used is just inheriting someone's problems.

**Family Comes First**

8. Whatever you want, dear.
9. I just want my kids to have it better than I did.
10. But that new RV will help our family bond.

**I'll Do It Later (I Promise.)**

11. We'll pay it when the tax return comes in.
12. I'll start my budget next month.
13. I'll worry about the future when it gets here

**Debt's Not So bad, Right?**

14. If everyone stopped borrowing money, the economy would fail.
15. I must be able to afford it if I was approved for the loan.
16. I need a house payment for tax purposes.

**I Earned This.**

17. You're only young once, right?
18. But we're on vacation.
19. I work hard, I deserve it.

**Poor, Pitiful Me.**

20. Why make more money? Uncle Sam will just take it all away.
21. The little man can't get ahead.
22. If I earn too much, I'll lose my public assistance.

**No Worries, I'm Covered**

23. My rich grandparents are going to leave me money.
24. I can't afford Insurance  But hey, my weed eater has a three year extended warranty.
25. It's okay, I have overdraft protection.

A lot of us are afraid to succeed either because of Family Background, the poor state we're in right now or we're afraid to step out of our comfort zone. I would say to you: step out of your comfort zone, send fear packing, and just picture yourself as being successful. Mojo is an example of a person who played Professional Basketball for a living and thought that he'd always have money because he was good in sports. The problem here is that he has to always remain in good physical shape. If Mojo breaks an arm or leg, his career might be over and he won't have a back-up plan.

## Forty Years and A Gold Watch or You Need to Provide Your Own Golden Parachute

Many of you are very traditional in your thinking and there is nothing wrong with that if it doesn't stunt your intellectual growth. We believe that you go to school and finish college and obtain a good job. Also, that you should start this job around the age of twenty and work on the job for about forty years.

A lot of companies and corporations aren't very loyal to their employees. Many employees buy into the stock option plans on certain jobs and place a lot of their hard earned money into the stocks of the company. A lot of employees end up with the company going belly-up and losing everything. I've seen the news reports of employees on TV crying because they were comfortable at the workplace and had put all of their savings into the stocks, bonds, 401-K Plans, etc., but ended up with nothing. In my personal opinion, when a company goes belly-up and loses all of the employees' savings, any monies left should be split among affected employees according to their contributions.

It is time for employees to take their Retirement into their own hands. Find yourself a good solid investment and plan your own future. The best time to start investing is when you're eighteen to twenty years old. However, you might be thinking, *I'm much older than twenty years old now*. Well, start where you are right now by finding a solid stock or mutual fund to invest in. You've taken a positive step when you bought this step-by-step guide that will lead you through the steps to start your own investment club. Whatever decision you make right now will probably determine whether you will end up like Bill or Will. Now Bill is an example of a man who invested wisely over the years and is cruising into his Retirement. On the other hand, Will is an example of a man who let the years pass without keeping track. Now, he's wondering how he will survive on his retirement. Last of all, you certainly don't want your cries for help in your old age to be like some invisible person talking into a microphone. This will be like being in a valley between mountain tops, crying for help and no one can hear you. The only sound will be your very own echo bouncing between the mountains.

On a brighter note, most of you probably haven't reached this point yet. You have time, so use it wisely and start putting monies aside for your retirement. I'm speaking of retirement because not all of you will want to start an investment club. One thing for sure, you are going to retire one day, whether it be through having your financial matters in order so you can retire or age forces you to retire. It wont be wasted time, just decide how much you will need for your retirement and start working towards it. If you have no idea how much you will need for your retirement, there are financial planners, accountants, and other persons <u>well versed</u> in financial matters who can assist you. So, don't be afraid, don't procrastinate, and DO IT NOW!

## When to Start Investing

You know, poverty is a generational thing, just like wealth. Some people are born wealthy and become poor through waste and over indulgence. Other people are born poor and become wealthy because someone introduced them to financial planning when they were young. There are still others who had parents, relatives or friends who were smart investors and started them from the day they were born and taught them through the years.

I've developed a plan which I think is simple for anyone to follow. If you're expecting a child, find a good solid mutual fund or stock to invest in for your child. You will only have to invest a small amount each month: your goal is for your child to retire at an early age.

## The early Retirement Plan is in three stages:

(1) Start investing when your child is born and invest for 240 months or twenty years. If you invest in the right Mutual Fund or stock, the child can Retire at twenty years old.
(2) If your Financial Goal for your child is not reached at twenty years, set the next Retirement goal at 480 months or forty years.
(3) Last of all, if you don't feel you have enough retirement money at forty years, set next the Retirement Goal at sixty years. During these Retirement Planning Phases, you will study the market, diversify your funds, and use leveraging to maximize your retirement funds. I know you're probably thinking that twenty years is a long time. Also, you might say, "I don't want to think about twenty forty or sixty years". Guess what? Most people in the United States will waste those twenty forty and sixty years and not have any money for their retirement when they become of age.

I know that it's hard thinking long term but why not put a small amount of money into a good stock or mutual fund while those years are slowly passing by? You might say that you're not young anymore or that all of your children are grown. Well, my answer to that is that you can start right where you are right now.

The hardest part for you whether you're young or old is to be committed. Sometimes we get so comfortable in our comfort zones that we're afraid to do anything different. I know you might be hesitant or afraid, but you have to think about what "courage" is. "courage" is doing what you know is right even though you are afraid.

Answer this question for me: would you rather be afraid and do nothing about your finances until your Retirement Age? Or, would you rather take a chance on a good stock or Mutual Fund until your Retirement Age while you are afraid? I truly believe that the latter will cause you to reap financial rewards beyond your wildest dreams. Come on, put your fears behind you and take this trip with me to "Financial Freedom." I forgot to tell you that it's alright to be afraid but you must have a "Positive Attitude."

Sam is an example of a man who invested from the time he was young. He also diversified over the years: now, he's headed for one of his vacation homes. Vickie is another example of a lady who is very young but is seriously thinking about investing. She's on the right track if she doesn't get side-tracked or discouraged. Julia is an example of a lady who came from a family of investors. Her parents started investing for her from the time she was born. She will have worries in life but not money worries.

Now, take a look at the Birth to Retirement Chart I developed (in Appendix A). It shows the stages of Retiring early (twenty years, forty ears or sixty five years). This example shows that by investing $500.00 a month for sixty five years, you will have $390,000.00 (this is not including interest you've earned). If you can't invest $500.00 a month, invest what you can but be consistent.

## Do I Go IT Alone After the Club Is Started?

After you've gotten your investment club off the ground, you might feel like you don't have enough information at your disposal. My book will get you set up and running without any problems. I can't tell you which stocks, bonds or mutual funds to pick. I've said this before, if your club is thinking seriously about a particular fund to invest in, there is nothing better than doing your homework. What I mean is: gather such information like: how long has the fund been in existence? What kind of interest rate did it pay for the last year, the past three and five years? What type of companies are involved in this fund? What's the minimum investment price? As I've said earlier, get a prospectus and read about the fund. Also, there are agencies out there that can help you, such as the NAIC and the AAII.

Take a look at this example about Paula who just sits around wondering what stocks or mutual funds to invest in. Use the information above to your advantage. You will reap rewards far above anything you can imagine.

## Where Do I Get the Money to Invest?

You might be thinking: *I want to invest in the stock market or I want to start an investment club but where will I get the money?* You might also feel that the little income you have now is taxed to the breaking point. Also, you might say that you don't have any money to put in a savings account, not to mention investing. I have some good news for you—: consider giving yourself a raise on the job where you work now. All you have to do is increase your number of exemptions on your W-4 form for your federal and state taxes; This will put more money in your take home pay. Let's say you're claiming Married and 0 and you get a big refund when you file your taxes. Why not increase your exemptions on your W-4 form to get your refund all during the year?

Another thing you can do is set up a budget. One thing a budget will do is tell how much money you make (income) and where the money is going. A budget will cause you to eliminate waste and get control over your income (you must use it though). By doing the things I've just mentioned, you'll start to see a surplus in your take home pay. If you take only ten percent of the surplus and invest it, you'll begin to see a brighter financial future.

Once you start making money from investments, you'll get excited and want to invest more. I've told you where to get the extra money to invest. The thing to do now is not procrastinate, but to do it now so you can realize some of the many possibilities that can happen in your life.

Patricia is an example of a lady who is interested in investing but doesn't have any money. She doesn't have any savings and she's lived a life of spend it as fast as she makes it. Patricia needs to first of all look at the sample budget in (Appendix A). The Willis Family is a ficticious family

budget that was tailored after the author's family budget. It is based on a one income family. The money is paid via direct deposit on a bi-weekly basis. The Willis Family included just about everything you can think of. Also, pay particular attention to the fact that they had a surplus of $6.00 after everything was paid.

After carefully reviewing it, Patricia needs to develop her own budget to get a handle on where her money is going. Patricia doesn't need to think about the income of the Willis Family, because they had a larger monthly income than her. Also, she gets paid once a month. She can only make a budget based on the net income she brings home.

## Saving Is easy, Commitment is hard

Think about this, from the time a child is born, if you only save $8.34 a month you would have $100.08 at the end of a full year (in Appendix A): This is a small amount and wouldn't hurt any family that works. When the child reaches twelve years of age, you would have $1,200.96 for that child. How many of us now have twelve year olds and have put aside $1,200.96 for them? Probably very few of us have done this. Yes, it's easy because it's such a small amount. Here's where the problem comes in, are you going to do it? Look at something else, if you were to save this $8.34 a month for twenty years, the child would have $2,001.60 by the time he or she reaches twenty years of age. Most people are not going to do it. Most people are going to sit around and watch the child grow up and not save a cent for the child or have the child save anything.

It takes twenty one days of continuous effort for anything to become a habit. Think about the things that are important to you. You do those things without thinking. But when you really stop to think about it, a lot of things in life are generational in nature. Let's look at obesity in families. Many people will say, "I just have big bones." They never look at eating habits. Another generational thing is poverty for the most part. Many of us will blame the system. For instance, "the man is holding me back." Another one, "they don't like me where I work so I can't move up." Have you ever heard the phrase, "it's not how much you make, it's what you do with what you make.?" Well, it's true, if you only make $300.00 a week, why would you spend $400.00 a week? One of the biggest problems is that we spend without keeping up with what we're spending. Then we get angry or upset when all of the money is gone and we don't know where it went. This further supports the necessity for a realistic, workable budget.

# START OUT THE RIGHT WAY AND YOUR CLUB WILL BE SUCCESSFUL

Whether you're talking about starting an investment club, social club or some prestigious type club, you have to think about the make-up of the club. You want people in your club or organization with similar values, thoughts and ideas. Everyone has a different personality and thank God for that! Can you imagine a World where all of our thoughts, values and ideas were the same? I can't either because it's the differences in all of us which make the World a beautiful and interesting place to live.

Whatever kind of club you're thinking about, I'm sure you have a picture in your mind of what you want it to look like. For instance, the goals of your club or organization have to be similar. You must agree on how many members you want in the organization. There has to be something concrete as to how long you want it to last. Some organizations have life time memberships as long as you meet certain requirements. Starting out the right way is very important:

Think on this example: If you want to make a cake, you must have certain ingredients: you must mix them up a certain way for a certain amount of time, you must cook it at a certain temperature for so many minutes. Under these same conditions, your cake will turn out basically the same each time. You have to be very careful in your selection of members for your club or organization.

Remember, the way you build it from the start is the kind of club or organization you're going to have. Look at some of the things below that I feel you must do from the very beginning:

### Recruiting the right club members

Anytime you are part of something great, it gives you a sense of belonging. This is a way in which you can develop new friendships and work towards securing your financial future. If you feel good about the organization, you want to share it with others. Well, in order to be effective in trying to persuade others to join your investment club, I feel that you must be equipped to talk about your club in terms of what it has to offer that would cause someone to want to join your club. Knowing what your club has to offer is not enough. You must have such great excitement about your club until whoever you're talking to can't imagine themselves not being in your club. There are many people from different organizations, clubs and corporations that you wouldn't be able to touch in terms of their knowledge about their organization. But if you have the one thing that most people lack when talking about their organization, people will be anxious about joining your club. The one thing would be "EXCITEMENT."

Think about it for a moment, you have Elementary School Teachers, High School Teachers, College Professors, Military Leaders, etc. who are knowledgeable about their profession. The ones I'm referring to can talk about their career or profession non-stop for hours. If you had a book on the subject which they were talking about and you could follow along, they could probably quote the book verbatim. For most of them, you will find that they will be missing the one ingredient that it takes to hold one's interest. You guessed it, they won't have any excitement about what they're talking about. I know you've heard the phrase, "Michael could sell ice to an Eskimo." The appeal for the buyer is not what Michael is selling, it's his EXCITEMENT about what he's selling. What I'm talking about here is, knowing what your club has to offer but more than that, putting yourself into what you're talking about. Talk about your club as though it were the most important thing on earth!

I remember when our club first started, I made up a fact sheet about our club and the Mutual Fund we purchased.

I call this the Financial Freedom ("FINFREE") Investment Club Recruiting Sheet. I would take this sheet with me and our 40 Year Investment Chart and just talk to people.

Everyone would get so excited just off of my excitement. You must get a feel for the commitment level of people who get excited and join your club right away. You can't allow them to join just because they're excited. If you do this, what you might have is a person who comes to one meeting, pays his/her dues and never come back. Based on my experience over the last few years, it's alright for a person to get excited and want to join your club right away. However, you might want to explain to the potential member it is alright to join the investment club. Also, explain that dues must be paid each month so the money can be combined into one lump sum to invest with American Century Investors. Others will take longer to make up their minds as to whether they want to join the club or not.

For example, I was talking to an Army Recruiter at my job. He wanted to join the investment club when I first talked to him, so I gave him some information to look over and told him that I would have to discuss it with my fellow club members. I got back with him and invited him to one of our weekly meetings. He never came to a meeting and he never said anything else about joining our investment club for an entire year. Get this, he took over a year to join the club; but today, he's the most committed member in our club and pays his dues faithfully every month.

Below, you will see some examples about investing:

Ned is an example of a person who is trying to get Josh to join his investment club. Josh is an example of a man who just lost his job and he's down on his luck. He's worried about how he's going to make ends meet (investing is the last thing on his mind). Now, Allen is an example of a man who is trying to convince Charlie that he's not too old to start investing.

REMEMBER: Don't get discouraged if people don't join your club right away. Remember, it's better to build your club slowly with the right level of commitment from the beginning.

## FINANCIAL FREEDOM ("FINFREE") INVESTMENT CLUB RECRUITING SHEET

I developed the information sheet below about our club so when club members are talking to people about joining the club, they can talk intelligently about the club. You can use the one I developed below or you can develop your own.

I'm happy you decided to meet with me today to talk about joining our investment club. I want you to know that you can become a Financial Being: That is, being able to buy the things you want to buy when you want to buy them. Also, being able to travel to places where some people only dream about, being able to live in the home of your dreams and much, much more!

Our investment club was formed on February 20, 1999 with seven people showing up for our first meeting and all seven people joined.

We started investing in the Growth Mutual Fund through American Century Investors, out of Kansas City, MO. During the year 2001, the Stock Market started going south real fast. At that time, we switched to the Inflation Adjusted Treasury Fund (going from aggressive growth to a low risk fund). You will have to decide your level of risk. However, when stocks go down, that's not necessarily a bad thing. If you're in a good, solid fund, you will buy more stocks because it will go back up.

Now, a little more about the Mutual Fund Company we invest in. We invest with American Century Investors which started out as Twentieth Century Investors: It combined with the BENGHAM Group to form American Century Investors. It started out with just two Mutual Funds, with assets of $100,000.00. The founder is Mr. James E. Stowers. This information can be verified in James Stowers Book, "Yes you can achieve financial independence" (the book is in the Bibliography).

Currently, American Century has been in business for over forty years and manages over 100 billion dollars in total assets. It offers over seventy mutual funds to invest in and it invests in over sixteen thousand companies. If you invest with us, you will be investing in NO Load Mutual Funds (you don't have to pay to invest or withdraw). "Loaded Mutual Funds " (you have to go through a broker to invest and withdraw and you have to pay each time).

When I was learning the mutual fund business 25 years ago, there were two separate and distinct types of funds: load and no load.

Load funds were those that charged a commission, which compensated the broker who put the client into the fund. This commissions took different forms – front load, back load, etc. – but the main point was the investor was going to pay a typically one-time fee for the advice they were getting in selecting funds, and the load was the mechanism used to pay the broker (indirectly, via the fund) for that advice.

No load funds were those funds sold without any commission, and they were a revelation to individual investors. They effectively de-coupled the process of getting investment advice., as investors could pick their own no-load funds and buy them either directly from the mutual-fund company itself, or a bit later on, through the mutual-fund supermarkets that appeared at Schwab and Fidelity.

This ability to "cut out the middleman" was a huge deal to investors during the 1980's and 1990s and spurred the creation of a vast "do it yourself" industry of newsletters (including SMI), books, and other educational materials designed to help guide investors as to how they could invest on their own.

For those on the no-load side of the fence, the idea of paying 5% or more off the top when buying mutual funds seemed like a ludicrous idea, no matter how many charts were produced by commission-based brokers showing that it was actually a reasonable deal. But the one bummer of being a no-load fund investor was there were certain families of mutual funds that we often wished we could have access to, but couldn't because they were exclusive to the load/advisor camp.

At the head of this list was the American Funds Group. They have long been the biggest, and more subjectively, at least among the best funds that the load camp had to offer.

Which is why this week's news that the American Funds are making all of their funds available without/loads via Schwab and Fidelity is such big news. To grizzled observers of the decades-long mutual fund Cold War, this is the Berlin Wall Event. The underlying structure underpinning load funds has been crumbling for years and the system has obviously been dying a slow death. But this is the visible event that elicits the "Wow, I never thought I'd see the day reaction "

The End of an Era: American Funds Goes No-Load_1 Sound...

https//soundmindinvesting:com/articles/view/the-end-of-an-era...

At any rate, we'll focus on the good news as we conclude this lesson, and the good news is that no-load fund investors now have access to the American Funds, a fund family that has long produced excellent results for investors at reasonable ongoing costs.

Think back to the time when you first began to walk. No matter how many times you fell down, you would always get up and try again. Isn't it amazing as we get older, if we fail at one thing, we're ready to give up! Well, don't fail to join our investment club because remember, there is strength in numbers. We're working towards getting twenty committed members. Banks believe in numbers and that's why they try to get as many depositors as possible. Once the bank gets your money, they will pay you one or two percent and invest your money for a much higher interest rate. This is what our club does through American Century, getting a much higher interest rate.

You know why most people don't invest. Well, because everyone is so afraid of losing money. But you know, there are only a few sure things in life.

## DEATH
## TAXES
## TIME

The one we like to talk about most is time because time will continue whether we're here or not. Investing is like that too, once you invest your money, it will continue to make money for you whether you do anything or not over time. You can either use time on your side or just let it slip away, like most people do. The best time to invest is when you're eighteen to twenty years old or younger, but it's never too late.

I feel like Mr. James Stowers when he said, "My job is not to tell you what you should do but to make you aware of what you can do! This quote came from James Stowers' book, "Yes you can . . . Achieve Financial Independence."

Every person wants to become financially independent but as Mr. STOWERS says:

> "It's not going to be easy and it's not going to happen by accident! It will come as a result of not being controlled by circumstances, being determined that nothing will prevent you from accomplishing your goals, your determination to increase your knowledge through study, experience, continuous effort and by helping other people become successful and they in turn will help you become successful."

## You Must Obtain a Tax Identification Number from the IRS

Since your investment club is just getting off the ground, this would be the perfect time to get a Form SS-4 from the IRS. This form is an Application for an Employer Identification Number (EIN). This is a nine- digit -number (example – 123456789) assigned to employers, sole proprietors, corporations, partnerships, estates, trusts, certain individuals, and other entities for tax-filing and reporting purposes. You can obtain this form from www.irs.gov. It's a simple form to fill out (the instructions are on the back of form to show you what goes in each space), so get this done, keep a copy and send the original to the IRS. It will only take a few weeks to receive your Tax ID

Number. Secure this Tax ID Number in a safe place so you can always find it. The reason being, you will use this Tax ID Number on all of your transactions for your club.

IRS EIN SS-4 Forms are Here / www1.ein-gov.us
www.ein-gov.us/step-by-step/Application

AdGet a Federal EIN Number from the IRS Today. Secure Online IRS FEIN Appication. GovSimplified is a document preparation & Filing Service and Cannot provide legal.ein-gov.us has been visited by 10K + users in the past month.

## Certificate of Assumed Names form must be obtained from the Register of Deeds

Once you talk to a group of people or just two or three people who are interested in joining your investment club, they will have to sign a Certificate of Assumed Names Form. You can get this form from your Register of Deeds (you can get several copies and make as many copies as you want). The members will have to put their addresses on this form also. Next, you will need to see a Notary Public who will have to list all of the partners on this form, sign the form, and affix his/her signature and seal on the form. Now, you're ready to take the form to the Register of Deeds to pay the registration fee (probably about $8.00 to $10.00) to get the partners registered). The Register of Deeds will give you a copy for your record. In two or three weeks, you will receive a copy of your form showing the Register of Deeds' name, county, when your form was presented, and recorded, the date and time, which book it's recorded in, and page number. Keep this with all of your records for the club. You get the club's name registered because it's the law and you will be operating illegally if not registered. Not being registered could cause your club to be liable for a lot of unnecessary fines. It's best to do things right from the very beginning. Who knows, your club might grow to be very big one day (maybe to the tune of millions of dollars). You would certainly want things in order to the benefit of all involved prior to this.

## A PARTNERSHIP AGREEMENT MUST BE DRAWN UP ONCE YOU GET MEMBERS TO JOIN YOUR CLUB

The Partnership Agreement explains how the club will operate (see below). If you have any questions about anything regarding the investment club, you should be able to find it in the Partnership Agreement. You can use a Partnership Agreement from another club that's already in operation. THOMAS O'HARA and KENNETH S. JANKE SR wrote a book entitled: **"How to start and run a Profitable Investment Club."** Thomas E. O'Hara and

Kenneth S. Janke, Sr. were top officers of the National Association of Investors Corporation (NAIC). Thomas E. O'Hara was the chairman of NAIC and Kenneth S. Janke, Sr. was the president and CEO of NAIC.

Since 1951, NAIC has provided investment education for individuals and clubs. I decided to pattern our club's Partnership Agreement after the one in O'HARA'S and JANKE'S book. Of course, I did make many changes to the agreement that were tailored more to fit our club. However, it would be better if the agreement had input from all of the club members. Also, I believe that the agreement should be reviewed at least once a year. There may be times when changes will dictate a review earlier. All partners will have to sign, date, and put their addresses on the agreement. Take a look at our club's Partnership Agreement below:

Partnership Agreement of the Financial Freedom ("FINFREE") Investment Club ® of North Carolina

This Partnership Agreement is effective February 20, 1999 by and between the Partnership listed below:

**(NAME OF ALL PERTNERS)**

All partners listed above agree to the following:

1. **FORMATION:** The partners above form a General Partnership in accordance with and subject to the laws of the State of North Carolina.

2. **NAME:** The name of the Partnership shall be Financial Freedom ("FINFREE") Investment Club ® of North Carolina.

3. **TERM:** The Partnership will begin on February 20, 1999 and will continue until December 31$^{st}$ each year and will continue each year after that unless earlier terminated.

4. **PURPOSE:** To invest the assets of the Partnership in Mutual Funds, Stocks, and other securities for the Retirement, Education, and Benefit of the Partners.

5. **MEETINGS:** Periodic meetings will be held monthly or as determined by the Partnership.

6. **INITIAL AND FUTURE CONTRIBUTIONS:** The Partners will make initial contributions to the Partnership in the amount of at least $110.00 per month on the date of each meeting. Shares to be invested will remain the same for one year, ending December 31$^{st}$. The amount to be in-

vested by each club member will increase by $5.00 each year for a period of 40 years. When the number of members reach twenty, no member can own any more than 20% of the total Shares authorized for the club (example: 20 divided by 100 = .20 percent).

7. **CLUB'S WORTH:** The club's assets minus liabilities will be determined on a regularly scheduled date and time set by the Partnership.

8. **HOW SHARES ARE MAINTAINED:** Shares will be maintained in the name of each partner. Each partner's Shares Contribution to, or Shares Withdrawal from the Partnership, will be credited or debited to that partner's Share Account.

9. **MANAGEMENT OF THE CLUB:** Each partner will participate in the management and conduct of affairs of the Partnership in proportion to the value of his/her Shares except as otherwise determined.

10. All decisions will be made by the partners, whose Shares total a majority of the total Shares of all the partners.

**11. PROFIT AND LOSSES:** Shall be in proportion to the number of Shares (% owned).

**12. REVIEWING OF THE CLUB'S BOOKS:** Books will be kept on all transactions. Books will be available for any partner to review at any time.

**13. CONDITION OF THE CLUB:** At the end of each Calendar Year, all members will be made aware of the profits/losses of the club. This tells how well the club has done for the whole year. The club also gets Quarterly Statements so each partner can tell how the club is doing on a Quarterly Basis.

**14. BANK ACCOUNT:** The Partnership may select a bank for the purpose of opening a Checking Account. Funds in the bank account will be withdrawn by checks signed by a partner designated by the Partnership. The bank account will also be used for automatic withdrawals of funds to purchase Mutual Funds to whatever Mutual Fund Company the Partnership chooses. The automatic withdrawal will be on a certain date each month as determined by the Partnership.

**15. NO COMPENSATION:** No partner will be compensated for services rendered to the partnership, except reimbursement expenses

**16. ADDITIONAL PARTNERS:** Additional partners will be admitted at any time, upon unanimous consent of all the partners, so long as the number of partners does not exceed twenty percent.

**17. TRANSFER OF A PARTNER'S SHARES:** No partner can transfer his/her Shares to another account. However, any partner can withdraw funds from his/her Shares after presenting a written request to the Partners. However, a $10.00 penalty will be taken from that partner's Share Account.

**18. REMOVAL OF A PARTNER:** Any partner may be removed by agreement of the partners whose Shares total a majority of the value of all partners Shares. Written notice of a meeting where removal of a partner is to be considered shall include a specific reference to this matter. The removal will become effective upon payment of the removed partner's Shares.

**19. TERMINATION OF THE PARTNERSHIP:** The Partnership will be terminated by the agreement of the partners whose Shares total a majority in value of all the other partners. A written notice to terminate the Partnership will be given to all partners. All liabilities of the Partnership will be met at this time and payment will be made to all partners or their designated representative in check form for the total amount of Shares they own.

**20. VOLUNTARY WITHDRAWAL (PARTIAL OR FULL) OF A PARTNER'S SHARES:** Any partner may withdraw a part or all of his/her Shares and the Partnership will continue as a Taxable Entity. The partner withdrawing a portion or all of his/her Shares will give a written notice to the Secretary. The written notice will be considered to be received as of the next meeting of the Partnership.

**21.** A General Partner will make a phone call to the Mutual Fund Company or use the Internet to determine the total value of the withdrawing partner's Shares. The General Partner will have the Mutual Fund Company to do a Wire Transfer (ACH) to the Partnership's local bank account. After which, a check will be made out to the withdrawing partner for their total Shares. An

ACH Wire Transfer will be used because it doesn't cost the withdrawing partner or the club any extra money.

## 22. DEATH OR INCAPACITY OF A PARTNER:

In the event of the death or incapacity of a partner, receipt of notice of such an event will be treated as notice of full withdrawal of that partner's Shares. The partner's Shares will be paid to whoever is designated as the beneficiary.

## 23. TERMS OF PAYMENT:

Anytime a partner wants to withdraw partial or all of his/her Shares, a check is the only means by which they will be paid. Payment will be the same as specified in number 19 above.

## 24. FORBIDDEN ACTS: NO PARTNER WILL:

a. Bind or obligate the Partnership to any extent whatsoever with regard to any matter outside the scope of the Partnership.
b. Assign, transfer, pledge, mortgage or sell all or part of his interest in the Partnership to any other person whomsoever, or enter into any agreement as the result of which any person not

      a partner shall become interested with him/her in the Partnership.

  c. Purchase an investment for the Partnership where less than the full purchase price is paid for it.

  d. Use the Partnership's name, credit or property for other than Partnership purposes.

  e. Do any act detrimental to the interests of the Partnership for which would make it impossible to carry on the purpose of the Partnership.

This agreement of the Partnership shall be binding upon the respective beneficiaries of the partners.

The partners have caused the agreement of the Partnership to be executed on the dates indicated above, effective as of the date indicated above.

**NAME:** _____

**NAME:** _____

**NAME:** _____

**NAME:** _____

**NAME:** _____

**NAME:** _____

## ACCOUNTING FOR MONIES DONATED

Whether you meet as a club weekly, monthly or quarterly, you must have some method of tracking monies and giving credit to club members when they pay their dues. The Contribution Form I developed (Appendix A), is an excellent way to keep up with monies that each club member pays each month when our club meets. When we first started the club, I did a lot of worrying about how I was going to keep up with the monies paid by each member. I looked at different accounting methods by other clubs but I wanted something different. I also wanted a form that was simple, where anybody could accurately keep up with club member's dues.

I grew tired and weary trying to figure out how I would account for the monthly dues. So, I prayed about it and it was revealed to me to design the Contribution Form (Appendix A). I think if we can always remember who is in control of us, we won't become tired and discouraged. We must try to remember and reflect on God's Words in Galatians 6:9 (NASB), which says, "Let us not lose heart in doing good, for in due time we will reap if we do not grow weary." The form has a note on it showing where an Administration Fee was paid by each member when the club started out. I was able to find a bank that has Free Checking. Club members no longer have to pay an Administrative Fee (which was used for bank service charges in the past).

I'm glad that we have money as a medium of exchange. Can you imagine having an investment club where we were still under the Bartering System? **I can see it now, you're having a meeting with your club members and they're paying their club dues (one person pays dues with a donkey, another with an axe handle, and still another with chickens). It would not only be hard but impossible to account for their contributions equally.**

# SETTING UP YOUR CLUB TO RUN LIKE A WELL OILED MACHINE

I know that you've heard the phrase, "If you start out the right way, it will end the right way." No matter how you look at it, that's a true statement. Let's say you sign up a lot of members in your investment club However, you don't have it organized or you don't have any plans in place. Well, if you don't organize it before you start bringing members in, your club is heading for disaster.

**SAMPLE MONTHLY NEWSLETTER**

**FINANCIAL FREEDOM ("FINFREE") INVESTMENT CLUB ®**

**1234 Free Me Lane**
**Freedom, USA 00000-0000**
**(H) 000-000-0000**
**(W) 000-000-0000**

James P. Freedom  December 20, 2002
1957 Freedom Lane
Want Freedom, TX 00000-0000

Dear Club Member:

We're at the time of year when people have started celebrating Christmas with loved ones, eating delicious meals and beginning to exchange presents. A lot of you have traveled many miles to be with loved ones. I do hope that you and your Family will have a very Merry Christmas and that you will have a joyous and prosperous New Year. But remember the reason for the season, that CHRIST was born to save the World from sin.

You know, life is full of challenges: we're born and we have to learn to feed ourselves, learn how to walk, learn how to talk, learn that we have to go to school to educate ourselves, learn how to prepare for the job market, learn how to prepare for Marriage and a Family, learn how to trust GOD for all of our needs, learn how to prepare for Retirement, learn how to prepare for getting older, learn how to prepare for all types of illnesses, learn how to prepare for the final thing which is death. But of all the things we have to prepare for in life, if we don't learn to live and enjoy life on this earth the way GOD meant for us to, we will miss out on life.

All of us got on the Financial Freedom Bus on February 20, 1999. We started traveling on a journey to Financial Freedom.

Some are still on the bus but others have gotten off the bus. The Financial Freedom Bus is heading your way again in 2003. The bus will arrive at your location on April 15, 2003. Get on the bus and stay on the bus until you reach your desired level of Financial Freedom. Once you reach that level, you need to cash in your chips and enjoy the "Success" you've earned! I guess what I'm trying to do is get you to make a decision of commitment.

We haven't had a club meeting in the last couple of months. The reason for this is that the key leaders and I have gotten together to make some much needed changes in order to move forward. We've gone over our requirements and made some changes to bring about a level of commitment from everyone.

When you start out on a trip, you have to keep your eyes on the goal you've set or your destination. Also, don't compare yourself to others because you've set your own goals and that needs to be your focus. When we think of investing, we let "Fear" set in instead of believing that God wants us to be Financially Free. We're investing and learning about Financial Matters in order to be Financially Free one day.

But there will be a struggle along the way. Plus, stay in your lane. Every runner has to run at his/her own pace but don't grow weary and quit on us.

My father was famous for stating things as though they were fact. When I was very young, my father had a saying that goes like this, "If you take a hundred dollars and put it in the center of your hand and never open your hand, you will always just have that hundred dollars, but if you open up that hand and help somebody else, you will find that you will not only have that hundred dollars but it will begin to grow and multiply." I believe that my father was right because over the years, I've always gotten more by helping others. Try investing as a means of reaching your Financial Goals. You will not only be helping others but you'll also be helping yourself. There is an old saying, "If you keep doing the same thing and hoping to get different results, this is insanity."

As Einstein defined insanity… Albert Einstein, the German philosopher was born on March 14, 1879 and died on April 18, 1955. His definition of insanity was, "doing the same thing over and over and expecting different results."

[As Einstein defined insanity… - Columns … www.jamaicaobserver.com/columns/ As-Einstein-defined-insanity---12815922](http://www.jamaicaobserver.com/columns/As-Einstein-defined-insanity---12815922)

You've got to change the way you do things if you want your life to be different and better. You have to do this right away and not procrastinate because the longer you remain stagnant, the more you will become comfortable with doing nothing but wishing and hoping.

I'm enclosing a copy of the Revised Club Requirements listed below for everyone to be informed. They will take effect April 15, 2003. So, go ahead and make the change with us and your life will never be the same!

We're thinking of changing our Monthly Meetings to once a Quarter. The reason for this is that we get our Financial Statement once a Quarter (you can still mail in your Monthly Dues).

If you've gotten off the bus to financial freedom for some reason or the other, just get back on the bus on April 15, 2003 and stay on until you reach your desired level of Financial Freedom (you'll be so proud of yourself and I will too).

John C. Jones
President

# FINANCIAL FREEDOM ("FINFREE") ®
# INVESTMENT CLUB ® REQUIREMENTS

1. You can become a member of our investment club by adhering to a, b, or c below, along with the remaining requirements.

   If you want to become a member of our investment club, start attending meetings and pay $110.00 (will increase by $5.00 each year). And a one- time fee of $10.00 to get you registered with the Register of deeds. You will become a full-fledged member as long as you pay the $110.00 a month and abide by the Partnership Agreement Rules.

   At present, the club's bank account has free checking, so club members don't have to pay an administrative fee to cover service charges. Club members will have to pay an administrative fee, if it gets to the point the club can't find free checking at any bank.
2. Buy Shares each month. This is required towards building your Retirement.
3. Have an open mind.
4. Attend all meetings on time.
5. Bring your planner each time you attend a meeting.
6. Other responsibilities we would like for you to work on:

a. Assist in the recruitment of other members until our membership reaches twenty committed members.
b. Continue to educate yourself about investments and money matters.
c. Be a team player and work towards the good of the group.
d. Have a hunger and passion for building your Retirement.
e. Let your words and actions match each other.

## OPERATING PROCEDURES AND CLUB OFFICERS

The Operating Procedures list all of the Club Officers, their duties, information regarding inviting guests, when meetings are held, and how often, and method of notification about Monthly Meetings.

## OPERATING PROCEDURES AND DUTIES OF PARTNERS

These Operating Procedures were patterned after the ones in THOMAS O'HARA'S and KENNETH S. JANKE SR'S Book. After 24 months (March 01, 2001) and Annually thereafter in march, partners shall elect the following positions and assign duties as described below by a majority vote.

1. **PRESIDENT:** Preside over meetings, set meeting dates and locations, appoint committees, and see that resolutions passed by the Partnership are carried out.
2. **VICE PRESIDENT:** Takes the place of the president when the president is absent or incapacitated. Assign companies to report on at the club meetings to each partner and responsible for ensuring that the club's study program is properly carried out.
3. **SECRETARY:** To keep a record of the actions authorized by the partners and notify partners of meetings and other activities.
4. **TREASURER:** To keep a record of the club's receipts and disbursements and partners interest in the club. The Treasurer will give partners receipts for payments made, deposits the funds in the club's bank account, and prepare the club's Monthly Valuation Statements. He/she will see that the needed tax information is compiled and file the necessary reports.
5. **GUESTS:** Partners may invite guests to any meeting as long as advance clearance is obtained from the host of the meeting. When consideration is given to adding partners to the club under paragraph 16 of the club's Partnership Agreement,

anyone considered should've been a guest for at least two prior meetings.

6. **MEETINGS:** The club shall hold a meeting on the last Wednesday of each month or another time set by the club. Written Notice of each meeting shall be given to each partner by the secretary at least one week before the meeting. Special meetings may be called by the President upon similar notice to the other partners.

# INVESTMENT CLUB MEETING

## SET GOALS SO THE CLUB MEMBERS WILL KNOW WHAT YOU'RE AIMING FOR

Whether you're starting an investment club or some other type of company, you will need to set some goals for the organization. You can come up with these goals through a group brainstorming session or you can each make a list and meet as a group to fine tune them. Either way, once you finalize your list and put them in print, each of you will become very excited about them. It will take a lot of excitement plus dedication for the club to succeed.

Take a look at our investment club goals below. As you begin to set goals for your club, here are a few things I want you to think about. Think of it as though you're going on a success journey and here are some things you're going to need along the way:

(1) People who are willing to take the journey.
(2) People who are able to visualize a picture of where you're going.
(3) People who are able to touch other people's lives along the way.
(4) People who want to improve their quality of life.
(5) People who are tired of being stagnant and want to go to the next level.
(6) People who have a strong desire and want to experience success in the club.
(7) People who have a sense of purpose and are goal oriented.
(8) People who have a hunger to grow personally and are willing to change.
(9) And finally, people who have the strength to forget the past and focus on the future.

I do hope that these few pointers will help you in looking at the kind of people you want in your club. I included a copy of our club goals, so feel free to use them as a guide for your club.

# FINANCIAL FREEDOM ("FINFREE") INVESTMENT CLUB ® GOALS

1. Meet on a specified date every month.
2. Become 20 members strong NLT December 31, 2006 and stabilize at 10 committed members NLT December 31, 2010.
3. Contribute $110.00 (will increase by $5.00 each year) each month through December 31, 2010.
4. Have Retirement Security.
5. Save on Taxes.
6. Compound our Interest Rate.
7. Buy and sell Real Estate.
8. Learn about leveraging and compounding.
9. Double our money in the least amount of time by using Rule 72 (divide 72 by the number of years within which we want our money to double). Example, 72 divided by 36% = 2 years to double our money.
10. Invest on a monthly basis no matter how the market looks.
11. Reinvest all earnings.
12. Diversify to reduce risk.
13. Educate ourselves about money.

# LOCAL BANK ACCOUNT

When the club becomes official, club members need to agree on a local bank. The purpose of the bank is to deposit club dues, have a vehicle where your chosen Mutual Fund/Stock Company can draft specific amounts each month to invest, and pay bills acquired by the club.

When the funds are drafted each month, a representative from the company will give you a name of the person who invested your money, a tracking number, the date and time of your investment.

Set up a good filing system to keep up with all of the paperwork from your local bank (a three ring binder tabbed off in sections is a good choice). When our club first started, we searched around until we found a bank with the lowest Services Charges. At first, credit unions seemed to have the lowest Services Charges ($1.00 per month). However, through further searches, we found a bank that has no Services Charges.

Avoid Overdraft Charges by keeping accurate Accounting Records. Another helpful tip is to have checks mailed to club members who want to withdraw a part of their Shares. Sometimes, wire transfers can be costly but you can have the Mutual Fund/Stock Company to do an ACH Wire Transfer and it won't cost anything.

Use a bank as a means to an end. Alan is an example of a person who thinks that a bank is the only way to go and by investing, you will lose everything you have. Alan will still be getting a 1% or 2% return on his money while you can get anywhere from 6% to 18% or more in a good solid investment.

## WHICH MUTUAL FUND/STOCK COMPANY

The club can invest in a Mutual Fund Company or it can buy stock from a particular company like Wal-Mart, CP&L, Walt Disney, etc. These are only examples and I'm not trying to suggest these to you by any means. Whether you choose to buy Mutual Funds or Stocks from a company, you need to keep up with all of the paperwork.

All types of paperwork will be coming to you (receipts for your investments, receipts each time you buy stocks or Mutual Funds, Quarterly Statements, information on changes or updates, etc.).

Before you invest in either of the two I mentioned, you need to get a Prospectus and club members need to review it very carefully. Things you need to look for are: What interest rate did the company receive over a year's time frame? What was the interest rate for the previous three to five years? Are you investing in "LOADED" or "NO LOAD" FUNDS? What are the total assets of the company? What's the minimum initial investment?

You might be thinking right now, *"what particular Stock, Bond or Mutual Fund should I start with?"* The best thing that I can tell you is to go on the Internet and type in Investing and do a search. All types of investments companies or firms will pop up. Read about some that you think you might be interested in. Request a Prospectus, Quarterly, Yearly and the last five years' Financial Statements, and look at what types of companies they invest in.

I'm partial to American Century Investors myself. I'm partial because MR. STOWERS started the investment firm with just $100,000.00. Also, this firm caters to the small investors as well as the large investors.

Today, this investment firm manages over $100,000,000.00 in assets. Another piece of solid advice that I can give you is that solid wealth is built slowly over time. Don't be so quick to fall for the get rich quick investment schemes. Think about it, if everyone is honest with him or herself, he or she will admit that they've thought about being wealthy whether they've pursued it or not. I'm here to tell you that you can become wealthy through investing.

Some of the keys are: you have to pick the right investment and study the ups and downs of the Stock Market, Bond, and Mutual Fund Markets. Another thing is that you have to be willing to stick with it for the long term. If you're the type of person who always sells when the market is up, you'll lose out on buying more shares when the market is down.

If you're going to try and build your wealth through an investment club, you need team members who can see the dream, who are committed, who contribute each month no matter how the market looks. You also need to set goals on how much money you want to obtain through the club.

This way, you will know what you're aiming for. Finally, you need to have a selling point for your club's shares (if the shares go down below a certain level, you will sell). When you sell, you don't have to spend the money, you can invest in a better or safer fund.

Now, Charlie is an example of a person who heard about the "S" Fund and put a lot of his hard earned money into that fund. Not only that but he's trying to convince Rick to invest in the same fund. Rick is an example of a person who is not just taking a plunge just because of what he heard.

I think I can honestly say that Rick is going to do his homework before he invests his hard earned money. More of us should be like Rick.

You know, you could probably go on the street right now and find a wino who could tell you how to make a million dollars. But would you go with the person who tells you how to make a million dollars or would you listen to the advice of someone who's made a million dollars? I don't think I need to answer that for you, the answer is pretty clear which choice you should make.

James Brown summed it up perfectly in one of his songs regarding people who do a lot of talking with no action, *"Talking loud and saying nothing."*

You might feel anxious right now, but take your time and at least have the right information before you make an investment for your future.

## FORTY (40) YEAR INVESTMENT CHART

I came up with the forty year Investment Chart (Appendix A) to show you how much money twenty people could have at the end of 40 years by investing a certain amount each month. This chart has a 5% Inflation Rate built in. The way it works is, you start out with a $101.00 Investment each month by each club member and it increases just by as little as $5.00 per year for 40 years. Total amount that you would have at the end of 40 years is just what you've contributed.

When you consider the amount of interest you will earn, its mind blowing! If you just take this chart and show it to people, they get excited when they realize the possibilities.

The key is to start when you're about twenty years old. It's never too late to start but you'll have longer to build wealth the younger you start. When you read this, you might be thinking, *I'm much older than twenty years* . Twenty is the best age to start investing. The next best age to start is the age that you are right now. Just take time and use it on your side to help you build wealth.

Remember, by yourself it is very hard to build wealth. However, if you organize a team of committed people who can see the dream, you're on your way to building wealth.

## HOW MANY SHARES TO BUY?

If you're serious about buying Mutual Funds or stocks for your Retirement, you need to decide how many shares you want to purchase. It's a good idea to set a goal of how many total shares you want to buy before you Retire.

By coming up with a number of shares to buy before you Retire, you will know what you're trying to accomplish. Also, you will know how many shares you must buy each month to reach your goal. Naturally, the older you are when you start, the more shares you will have to buy to have a comfortable Retirement Income. I believe it will excite you once you set the goal and begin to work towards it.

## 30 DAY MUTUAL FUND OR STOCK COMPARISON CHART

As I've said earlier, if you always do the same thing and never look at anything different, you will never know about other possibilities. Also, you will never know what your club is capable of accomplishing.

You don't have to but you can take two or more stocks, bonds or mutual Funds that your club has researched and track their growth for thirty days . This thirty day study might give your club some ideas about diversifying your portfolio.

The books I've read recommend that you have at least five (5) funds in your portfolio. The 30 day study of certain stocks, bonds or Mutual Funds will give you an idea of whether the stocks or Mutual Funds are growing or not. It's no guarantee, so you can study the stocks or Mutual Funds for longer than 30 days. But what it boils down to is that you're going to have to make a decision eventually.

## MORE IS NOT ALWAYS BETTER

When you start thinking about how many total members you want in your investment club, you might think the more, the merrier. However, your club's membership should comprise members who have the same goals, aspirations and visions as you. Some people start thinking about big numbers and get carried away.

They start looking at things like: if the club had forty members and they only paid $100.00 each per month, the club could invest at least $4,000.00 a month. That sounds good in theory only because you know as well as I do that the more members you have, the harder it is to make decisions, all members won't be committed and other members won't pay dues at all some months.

I'll go even further, if you can get 40 people to commit to paying only $25.00 a month to invest, it would be rare. I'm speaking from personal experience regarding members of our club. There were once 12 members in our club. The club's goal at first was to have 20 committed members. After several years of finding out that out of the 12 members, only four (4) were committed. After-which, our club made some much needed changes. The four (4) committed members decided to buy the shares of the other eight (8) members who weren't committed. To this day, we've gained three (3) more committed members and we're up to seven (7) committed members and the club is in good standing and operating smoothly. So, when you start thinking about how many members you want in your club, refer to our club goals and if you can find members willing to abide by your club goals, you will have members who will join and help your club to progress and move forward. We're still open to receive new members.

# HOW TO KEEP THE CLUB MEMBERS MOTIVATED AND FOCUSED ON CLUB GOALS

## DESIGNATED PLACE AND TIME FOR PERIODIC MEETINGS

When our club first started, we would always meet in my home. After awhile, one club member suggested that we alternate from one club member's house to the next and so forth. However, that didn't seem to work out too well. Even though it was put out in the last meeting, some members would always call and ask, "Whose house are we meeting at this week?" Also, the attendance went down by doing it this way. I found out over a period of time that having a specific place and time to meet worked out better. Club members attended more frequently and contributed more money to their share account by meeting at a particular place and time. Once a quarter, our club would meet at a restaurant and eat, laugh, and have fun while we conducted our business affairs. Our club was able to talk to the leaders in one city about meeting in their building once a month. We wanted our meeting to be in an office with a telephone, fax, and copy machine. We were able to get all of this free of charge. Of course we had to find an office in a town that was convenient for all of the members. If you can't find an office that's free of charge and convenient for all club members, you might want to meet in one of the club member's homes. You don't want to take on added expenses. Show a genuine concern for club members and their families (this helps the morale). Keep in mind that everything can't be written in stone, have an agenda but people do have problems, so be flexible.

## AGENDA FOR EACH TIME THE CLUB MEETS TO CONSERVE TIME

Have you ever gone to a meeting where the people were late coming and not organized when they arrived? I'm here to tell you that it's not a pretty sight. Remember, you're going to have more than one leader for your club. There's no reason everyone should be late. One of the first parts of being organized is being on time. I learned from my father many years ago to always arrive 15 to 30 minutes early for everything. If you're designated to lead the monthly meeting, and you're going to be late, designate another leader to take charge. Require all of your club members to be on time. I've heard that when you're supposed to be at a specific place at a specific time, and you're not there, you're stealing the time of others. Enough about time, you get the point. Make sure you have a planned agenda for monthly meetings. I can recall going to certain meetings and the leader was fishing for words and things to say. It was evident that the leader hadn't prepared for the meeting. An agenda should include but is not limited to the following: show genuine concern for your club members and their families, find out whether there is any additional stress or burdens on your members, talk about old business, give updates on the things that were suppose to be accomplished, mark members that are present and absent, take up money and give receipts to members buying shares, conduct new business (this should include how shares are doing,), give a tentative time and date for the next meeting (will be followed by written notification), answer questions and dismiss).

## GUEST SPEAKERS WHO WILL COME AND SHARE THEIR SUCCESS STORIES

Try to always remember the phrase, "no man is an island." I don't know who originated this phrase. But I do know that it's a true statement. I've known people who do a particular job. They would say that there's no one who is better at doing the job than them. The truth is, no matter how good or great you are at performing your particular job, there's always someone, somewhere who is better and faster. What I'm getting at is, don't operate your club in a vacuum or in isolation. Even though you might have done a lot of research and you might be well read, there are other people and organizations out there who will be thrilled to help you. Remember, your club is just getting started. Your club can benefit from the experiences of any type of successful organization. I might caution you though, prior to soliciting the assistance of any organization, do your homework. Do research on the organization and study some of their success stories over a certain time frame.

Check out several organizations and ask to visit them and observe their operations. Once you're satisfied with your research, you might ask them to visit one of your club's scheduled meetings. At this time, they can share information on what to do as well as what not to do to be successful, as well as some of their success stories. I believe that this will excite and motivate your club members. Your members will learn of some of the obstacles your speaker had to encounter and overcome prior to reaching his/her goals.

## DESIGNATED SPEAKER AT THE CLUB'S MEETING

## SPECIAL EVENTS WHERE FAMILY MEMBERS ARE INVITED

I know you've heard that the Family is what keeps most people going in life. Well. There are so many attacks on Families nowadays. There are questions going around like, "Is the Family Unit as we know it becoming extinct?' Or, "Is the Family Unit of old the only Family Unit where there is mother, father and children?" Well my Family consists of myself, my wife and my children. I'm incomplete when I'm away from my Family for extended periods of time. When you get ready to start your club, I'm sure the start up will go better if you have the support of your Family. Keep your Family up to date as far as the progress and operation of the club. Clubs that have been around for a long time and are successful hold Annual Meetings. At this time, Family Members are invited to fellowship and learn of the club's progress. When we're having troubles, the family is the first place we turn to for support and understanding. Always keep your Family up to date on your club's operations. Give your club time to get on an even footing. Don't exaggerate, be honest about how the club is doing.

The club might not be where you want it but just make sure you're headed in the right direction in terms of where you want to end up.

## MAKE SURE THAT FAMILY IS INCLUDED

## ENSURE CLUB MEMBERS GET FINANCIAL STATEMENTS ON A REGULAR BASIS

It doesn't matter what stock, bond or Mutual Fund you invest in, Financial Statements will be mailed to you on a periodic basis. All of the investment agencies our club partners with send out Quarterly Statements. Your statements will more than likely be on a Quarterly Basis also. When you get your statements, they will show the total monies invested for the current Quarter. The statements will also show the percentage of growth for the Quarter. Keep up with these Quarterly Statements so you will be able to track your fund's growth over the years. If your fund hasn't grown in a certain amount of years, you might want to look at some other funds. Be sure to give the fund an adequate amount of time to experience growth. Also, look at how you first invested in the fund. I'm referring to whether you invested for the Long Term Growth or the Short Term Growth. If you invested for the Long Term Growth, it takes five (5) or more years. On the other hand, if you invested for the Short Term Growth, you must give the fund 3 to 5 years.

You must be aware of the ups and downs of the Stock Market. A lot of people rush to sell when the market starts going south. But if you know that you're invested in a solid growth fund, take advantage of the ups and downs of the Stock Market. As your fund goes south, you will still have the same number of shares. It would be wise to purchase more shares so when the market goes back up, your fund will make money and you're steadily increasing your number of shares. Don't be so quick to sell when your fund goes up either. Make sure you're strong enough to withstand the ups and downs of the Stock Market.

# WHAT TO DO IF A MEMBER DIES OR BECOMES INCAPACITATED?

Your shares in the investment club should be valuable to you. Family should be made aware of how many shares you have in the club. Many American Citizens have died with no Family Member or friend having access to their money or assets. Our club has a Designation of Beneficiary Form so if a club member dies or becomes incapable of handling their Financial Affairs, they're covered. There is also a Contingency Beneficiary Form in case the first one dies before the club member. In all honestly we must be prepared when unfortunate events occur in our lives. As I mentioned earlier, there are some things that we have no control over. The three that come to mind right away are: death, taxes and time. Out of the three, we'll talk about death. If you don't put some safety net in place where Families of club members are taken care of, you're not looking after your club members. If you use the form that our club uses, make sure you update it from time to time. I was in the Military and I saw instances where a husband had his wife as his beneficiary. This husband got divorced but failed to change his beneficiary. He later remarried, was sent off to War and was killed in a Combat Zone. The first wife that he was divorced from got all of his insurance proceeds. This is a true story but very sad, so don't allow this to happen to your club members. You could run into a situation like Chris on the following page. His father died and hadn't designated a beneficiary.

## WHO WILL HANDLE YOUR AFFAIRS WHEN YOU'RE INCAPACITATED?

# FIND AN ORGANIZATION WHO THAT WILL DO THE CLUB'S TAX RETURNS

Investments clubs are not exempt from doing and filing Income Tax Returns. Our club has been very fortunate. At the end of our first year, I was wondering which agency I would get to do our taxes and how expensive it would be. I checked a number of tax agencies and found that it was quite expensive. There was a group of accountants who were right across the street from where I worked. I walked over and talked to the receptionist and asked if I could speak with one of the accountants. She stated that they were busy but if I could wait, she'll try to get me in. After awhile, one came out and I asked how much it would cost to do our club taxes. He asked, "Did you make any money during the year?" I told him that our club made $759.00 our first year. He took me into his office and showed me how to do the taxes for our club. He didn't charge me any money. He just said, "I don't mind helping a man who is honestly trying to make some money." I've been doing the club's taxes every year since then. I don't know whether you can find some agency that will do your taxes for free or teach you how to do your taxes for free or not. However, if you have to pay someone the first year, maybe someone in

"START A SUCCESSFUL INVESTMENT CLUB TO SECURE YOUR FINANCIAL FREEDOM AND RETIREMENT.

your club will learn how to do the club's taxes. If you don't really search around, you might run into someone like Joe on the following page. He's just looking for someone he can make a small fortune on.

John C. Jones
John.jones@Yahoo.com

# Bibliography

Charles J. Givens Financial Video Library, (1991), Your Personal Plan of Action, Powerful Investment Strategies, Tax Reducing Strategies and Personal Finance Strategies.

Charles J. givens, (1988), Wealth Without Risk, Publisher: Simon & Schuster, 1st edition.

Charles J. Givens, (1990), Financial Self-Defense – How to win the Fight for Financial Freedom, Publisher: Simon & Schuster, New York. New York.

Charles P.Conn, (1986), Promises to Keep (The Amway Phenomenon and How it Works), Publisher: Berkley Books, New York.

Dale Carnegie, (1936), How to Win Friends & Influence People, Publisher: Pocket Books, a division of Simon & Schuster, New York, New York.

Dr. Robert Anthony, (1984), Total Self Confidence,. Publisher: Berkley Books, New York.

James E. Stowers (1993), Yes, You Can - - - Achieve Financial Independence, Deer Publishing, Inc. Kansas City, Missouri, (1st edition).

Jerrold Mundis, ((1988), How to get out of Debt & Stay out of Debt & Live Prosperously, Pubisher: Bantom Books, New York, New York.

John C. Maxwell, (1978), Everyone Communicates Few Connect, Publisher: Thomas Nelson, Inc., Publishers, Nashville, Tennessee.

John C. Maxwell, (1979), Failing Forward. Publisher: Thomas Nelson, Inc., Publishers, Nashville, Tennessee.

John C. Maxwell, (1997), Your Roadmap for Success. Publisher: Thomas Nelson, Inc., Publishers, Nashville, Tennessee.

Kenneth M.Morris and Alan M. Siegel, (1993), Guide to Understanding Money & Investing. Publisher: Lightbulb Press, Inc., New York.

Mary K. Ash (1995), You Can Have it All, Publisher: Prima Publishing, Rocklin, CA

OG Mandino, (1968), The Greatest Salesman in the World. Publisher: Frederick Fell Publishers, Inc., Hollywood, FL.

Steve Crowley (1991), Money for Life, Publisher: Simon & Schuster, New York, New York.

Thomas E. O'Hara and Kenneth S. Janke, SR. (19960), Starting and Running a Profitable Investment Club. Publisher: Random House, New York.

Appendix A – Forms and Charts

Forty Year Investment Chart

Family Budget

Birth to Retirement Chart

Potential Club Members Chart

Form to Take Notes if Desired

Contribution Form for Monthly Dues

| FINANCIAL FREEDOM INVESTMENT CLUB 40 YEAR CHART | | | | | |
|---|---|---|---|---|---|
| CHART BASED ON 20 MEMBERS WITH A 5% INFLATION RATE BUILT IN | | | | | |
| ORIGINATED BY: JOHN C. JONES | | | | | |
| # | YEAR | INDIV MONTHLY AMOUNT | INDIV YEARLY AMOUNT | GROUP MONTHLY AMOUNT | GROUP YEARLY AMOUNT | GROUP TOTAL TO DATE |
| 1 | 1999 | 101 | 1212 | 2020 | 24,240 | 24,240 |
| 2 | 2000 | 106 | 1272 | 2120 | 25,440 | 49,680 |
| 3 | 2001 | 111 | 1332 | 2220 | 26.64 | 76,320 |
| 4 | 2002 | 116 | 1392 | 2320 | 27,840 | 104,160 |
| 5 | 2003 | 121 | 1452 | 2,420 | 29,040 | 133,200 |
| 6 | 2004 | 126 | 1512 | 2520 | 30,240 | 163,440 |
| 7 | 2005 | 131 | 1572 | 2620 | 31,440 | 194,880 |
| 8 | 2006 | 136 | 1632 | 2720 | 32,640 | 227,520 |
| 9 | 2007 | 141 | 1692 | 2820 | 33,840 | 261,360 |
| 10 | 2008 | 146 | 1752 | 2920 | 35,040 | 296,400 |
| 11 | 2009 | 151 | 1812 | 3020 | 36,240 | 332,640 |
| 12 | 2010 | 156 | 1872 | 3120 | 37,440 | 370,080 |
| 13 | 2011 | 161 | 1932 | 3220 | 38,640 | 408,720 |
| 14 | 2012 | 166 | 1992 | 3320 | 39,840 | 448,560 |
| 15 | 2013 | 171 | 2052 | 3420 | 41,040 | 489,600 |
| 16 | 2014 | 176 | 2112 | 3520 | 42,240 | 531,840 |
| 17 | 2015 | 181 | 2172 | 3620 | 43,440 | 575,280 |
| 18 | 2016 | 186 | 2232 | 3720 | 44,640 | 619,920 |
| 19 | 2017 | 191 | 2292 | 3820 | 45,840 | 665,760 |
| 20 | 2018 | 201 | 2412 | 4020 | 48,240 | 714,000 |
| 21 | 2019 | 206 | 2472 | 4120 | 49,440 | 763,440 |
| 22 | 2020 | 211 | 2532 | 4220 | 50,640 | 814,080 |
| 23 | 2021 | 216 | 2592 | 4320 | 51,840 | 865,920 |

| FINANCIAL FREEDOM INVESTMENT CLUB 90 YEAR CHART | | | | | | |
|---|---|---|---|---|---|---|
| CHART BASED ON 20 MEMBERS WITH A 5% INFLATION RATE BUILT IN | | | | | | |
| ORIGINATED BY: JOHN C. JONES | | | | | | |
| # | YEAR | INDIV MONTHLY AMOUNT | INDIV YEARLY AMOUNT | GROUP MONTHLY AMOUNT | GROUP YEARLY AMOUNT | GROUP TOTAL TO DATE |
| 24 | 2022 | 221 | 2652 | 4420 | 53,040 | 918,960 |
| 25 | 2023 | 226 | 2712 | 4520 | 54,240 | 973,200 |
| 26 | 2024 | 231 | 2772 | 4620 | 55,440 | 1,028,640 |
| 27 | 2025 | 236 | 2832 | 4720 | 56,640 | 1,085,280 |
| 28 | 2026 | 241 | 2892 | 4820 | 57,840 | 1,143,120 |
| 29 | 2027 | 246 | 2952 | 4920 | 59,040 | 1,202,160 |
| 30 | 2028 | 251 | 3012 | 5020 | 60,240 | 1,262,400 |
| 31 | 2029 | 256 | 3072 | 5120 | 61,440 | 1,323,840 |
| 32 | 2030 | 261 | 3132 | 5220 | 62,640 | 1,386,480 |
| 33 | 2031 | 266 | 3192 | 5320 | 63,840 | 1,450,320 |
| 34 | 2032 | 271 | 3252 | 5420 | 65,040 | 1,515,360 |
| 35 | 2033 | 276 | 3312 | 5520 | 66,240 | 1,581,600 |
| 36 | 2034 | 281 | 3272 | 5,620 | 67,440 | 1,649,040 |
| 37 | 2035 | 286 | 3432 | 5720 | 68,640 | 1,717,680 |
| 38 | 2036 | 291 | 3492 | 5820 | 69,840 | 1,787,520 |
| 39 | 2037 | 296 | 3552 | 5920 | 71,040 | 1,858,560 |
| 40 | 2038 | 301 | 3612 | 6020 | 72,240 | 1,930,800 |

# Family Budget

| WILLIS FAMILY BUDGET | | | | | | |
|---|---|---|---|---|---|---|
| DATE DUE | CHECK NUMBER | ACCOUNT OWED | AMOUNT PAID | DATE CLEARED | Payment Method |
| 20TH | | AAFEES | $300 | 2/24/2014 | Bank Draft |
| 5TH | | AAFMAA (JOHN) | 127 | | |
| 5TH | | AAFMAA (MAL) | 11 | | |
| 1ST | | AM HOME SHLD | 48 | | |
| 12TH | | ATT | 201 | | |
| 6TH | | CABLE (TIME WARNER) | 165 | | |
| 5TH | | COMFORT WIZARD | 21 | | |
| 15TH | | EMERGENCY FUND | 100 | | |
| 1ST | | INSURANCE (ANN) | 51 | | |
| 15TH | | FOOD | 500 | | |
| 1ST | | GAS (ANN) | 150 | | |
| 15TH | | GAS (JOHN) | 125 | | |
| 3RD | | GLOBE INSURANCE) | 56 | | |
| 1ST | | HOMEOWNERS ASSOC DUES | 40 | | |
| 19TH | | KEMPER | 164 | | |
| 1ST | | MALLORY | 89 | | |
| 1ST | | MORTGAGE (ASC) | 1302 | | |
| 4TH | | NG ASSOC | 25.79 | | |

| | | | | | |
|---|---|---|---|---|---|
| 27TH | | PROG ENERGY | 286 | | |
| 2ND | | PSNC | 83 | | |
| 1ST | | TITHES | 400 | | |
| 5TH | | TRICARE | 39 | | |
| 1ST | | VET (RAZEN) | 25 | | |
| 27TH | | WATER BILL | 145 | | |
| 15TH | | WELLS FARGO (CAR NOTE) | 470 | | |
| 1ST | | NEWS & OBSERVER | 20 | | |
| | TOTAL | | | | |

## Birth to Retirement Chart

| FROM BIRTH TO RETIREMENT CHART | | | |
|---|---|---|---|
| BY JOHN C. JONES | | | |
| YEAR OF BIRTH: | | | |
| YEARS TO RETIRE | FORMULA | DATE | BAL |
| 1 | 500 X 12 = 6000 | 01-01-2006 - 12-01-2006 | 6000 |
| 2 | 500 X 12 = 6000 | 01-01-2007 - 12-01-2007 | 12000 |
| 3 | 500 X 12 = 6000 | 01-01-2008 - 12-01-2008 | 18000 |
| 4 | 500 X 12 = 6000 | 01-01-2009 - 12-01-2009 | 24000 |
| 5 | 500 X 12 = 6000 | 01-01-2010 - 12-01-2010 | 30000 |
| 6 | 500 X 12 = 6000 | 01-01-2011 - 12-01-2011 | 36000 |
| 7 | 500 X 12 = 6000 | 01-01-2012 - 12-01-2012 | 42000 |
| 8 | 500 X 12 = 6000 | 01-01-2013 - 12-01-2013 | 48000 |
| 9 | 500 X 12 = 6000 | 01-01-2014 - 12-01-2014 | 54000 |
| 10 | 500 X 12 = 6000 | 01-01-2015 - 12-01-2015 | 60000 |
| 11 | 500 X 12 = 6000 | 01-01-2016 - 12-01-2016 | 66000 |
| 12 | 500 X 12 = 6000 | 01-01-2017 - 12-01-2017 | 72000 |
| 13 | 500 X 12 = 6000 | 01-01-2018 -12-01-2018 | 78000 |
| 14 | 500 X 12 = 6000 | 01-01-2019 - 12-01-2019 | 84000 |
| 15 | 500 X 12 = 6000 | 01-01-2020 - 12-01-2020 | 90000 |
| 16 | 500 X 12 = 6000 | 01-01-2021 - 12-01-2021 | 96000 |
| 17 | 500 X 12 = 6000 | 01-01-2022 - 12-01-2022 | 102000 |
| 18 | 500 X 12 = 6000 | 01-01-2023 - 12-01-2023 | 108000 |
| 19 | 500 X 12 = 6000 | 01-01-2024 - 12-01-2024 | 114000 |

| RETIRE NOW OR | LATER? | | |
|---|---|---|---|
| 20 | 500 X 12 = 6000 | 01-01-2025 - 12-01-2025 | 120000 |
| 21 | 500 X 12 = 6000 | 01-01-2026 - 12-01-2026 | 126000 |
| 22 | 500 X 12 = 6000 | 01-01-2027 - 12-01-2027 | 132000 |
| 23 | 500 X 12 = 6000 | 01-01-2028 - 12-01-2028 | 138000 |
| 24 | 500 X 12 = 6000 | 01-01-2029 - 12-01-2029 | 144000 |
| 25 | 500 X 12 = 6000 | 01-01-2030 - 12-01-2030 | 150000 |
| 26 | 500 X 12 = 6000 | 01-01-2031 - 12-01-2031 | 156000 |
| 27 | 500 X 12 = 6000 | 01-01-2032 - 12-01-2032 | 162000 |
| 28 | 500 X 12 = 6000 | 01-01-2033 - 12-01-2033 | 168000 |
| 29 | 500 X 12 = 6000 | 01-01-2034 - 12-01-2034 | 174000 |
| 30 | 500 X 12 = 6000 | 01-01-2035 - 12-01-2035 | 180000 |
| 31 | 500 X 12 = 6000 | 01-01-2036 - 12-01-2036 | 186000 |
| 32 | 500 X 12 = 6000 | 01-01-2037 - 12-01-2037 | 192000 |
| 33 | 500 X 12 = 6000 | 01-01-2038 - 12-01-2038 | 198000 |
| 34 | 500 X 12 = 6000 | 01-01-2039 - 12-01-2039 | 204000 |
| 35 | 500 X 12 = 6000 | 01-01-2040 - 12-01-2040 | 210000 |
| 36 | 500 X 12 = 6000 | 01-01-2041 - 12-01-2041 | 216000 |
| 37 | 500 X 12 = 6000 | 01-01-2042 - 12-01-2042 | 220000 |
| 38 | 500 X 12 = 6000 | 01-01-2043 - 12-01-2043 | 228000 |
| 39 | 500 X 12 = 6000 | 01-01-2044 - 12-01-2044 | 234000 |
| RETIRE NOW OR | LATER? | | |
| 40 | 500 X 12 = 6000 | 01-01-2045 - 12-01-2045 | 240000 |
| 41 | 500 X 12 = 6000 | 01-01-2046 - 12-01-2046 | 246000 |
| 42 | 500 X 12 = 6000 | 01-01-2047 - 12-01-2047 | 252000 |

| | | | |
|---|---|---|---|
| 43 | 500 X 12 = 6000 | 01-01-2048 - 12-01-2048 | 258000 |
| 44 | 500 X 12 = 6000 | 01-01-2049 - 12-01-2049 | 264000 |
| 45 | 500 X 12 = 6000 | 01-01-2050 -12 -01-2050 | 270000 |
| 46 | 500 X 12 = 6000 | 01-01-2051 - 12-01-2051 | 276000 |
| 47 | 500 X 12 = 6000 | 01-01-2052 - 12-01-2052 | 282000 |
| 48 | 500 X 12 = 6000 | 01-01-2053 - 12-01-2053 | 288000 |
| 49 | 500 X 12 = 6000 | 01-01-2054 - 12-01-2054 | 294000 |
| 50 | 500 X 12 = 6000 | 01-01-2055 - 12-01-2055 | 300000 |
| 51 | 500 X 12 = 6000 | 01-01-2056 - 12-01-2056 | 306000 |
| 52 | 500 X 12 = 6000 | 01-01-2057 - 12-01-2057 | 312000 |
| 53 | 500 X 12 = 6000 | 01-01-2058 - 12-01-2058 | 318000 |
| 54 | 500 X 12 = 6000 | 01-01-2059 - 12-01-2059 | 324000 |
| 55 | 500 X 12 = 6000 | 01-01-2060 - 12-01-2060 | 336000 |
| 56 | 500 X 12 = 6000 | 01-01-2061 - 12-01-2061 | 336000 |
| 57 | 500 X 12 = 6000 | 01-01-2062 - 12-01-2062 | 342000 |
| 58 | 500 X 12 = 6000 | 01-01-2063 - 12-01-2063 | 348000 |
| 59 | 500 X 12 = 6000 | 01-01-2064 - 12-01-2064 | 354000 |
| 60 | 500 X 12 = 6000 | 01-01-2065 - 12-01-2065 | 360000 |
| 61 | 500 X 12 = 6000 | 01-01-2066 - 12-01-2066 | 366000 |
| 62 | 500 X 12 = 6000 | 01-01-2067 - 12-01-2067 | 372000 |
| 63 | 500 X 12 = 6000 | 01-01-2068 - 12-01-2068 | 378000 |
| 64 | 500 X 12 = 6000 | 01-01-2069 - 12-01-2069 | 384000 |
| 65 | 500 X 12 = 6000 | 01-01-2070  12-01-2070 | 390000 |
| DEFINITELY RETIRE | NOW!!! | | |
| | | | |

## Potential Club Members Chart

## POTENTIAL INVESTMENT CLUB MEMBERS

| NAME/ CONTACT INFO | RELATIONSHIP |
|---|---|
| | |
| | |
| | |
| | |
| | |
| | |
| | |
| | |
| | |
| | |

# Form to Take Notes if Desired

## NOTES

START A SUCCESSFUL INVESTMENT CLUB TO SECURE YOUR FINANCIAL FREEDOM AND RETIREMENT

# Monthly Contribution Form

| FINANCIAL FREEDOM INVESTMENT CLUB "ORIGINATED BY JOHN C. JONES <br> CONTRIBUTION FORM / YEAR 2019      EQUITY INCOME / ONE CHOICE | | | | | | | |
|---|---|---|---|---|---|---|---|
| | CLUB | SHARE | SHARES | AMOUNT | SHARES | TOTAL | % OF |
| | MEMBER'S | PRICES | LAST | PAID | BOUGHT | SHARES | TOTAL |
| DATE | NAME | | MEETING | TODAY | TODAY | TODAY | SHARES |
| | | | | | | | |
| 1/8/2019 | Porky Pig One Choice Moderate | te$13.04 | 203 | $110.00 | 7.724 | 210.724 | |
| | | | | | | | |
| 2/12/2019 | Porky Pig One Choice Moderate | | | | | | |
| | | | | | | | |
| 3/1/2019 | Porky Pig One Choice Moderate | | | | | | |
| | | | | | | | |
| 4/1/2019 | Porky Pig One Choice Moderate | | | | | | |
| | | | | | | | |
| 5/7/2019 | Porky Pig One Choice Moderate | | | | | | |
| | | | | | | | |
| 6/1/2019 | Porky Pig One Choice Moderate | | | | | | |
| | | | | | | | |
| 7/1/2019 | Porky Pig One Choice Moderate | | | | | | |
| | | | | | | | |

| | | | | | | | |
|---|---|---|---|---|---|---|---|
| 8/10/2019 | Porky Pig<br>One Choice<br>Moderate | | | | | | |
| | | | | | | | |
| 9/5/2019 | Porky Pig<br>One Choice<br>Moderate | | | | | | |
| | | | | | | | |
| 10/3/2019 | Porky Pig<br>One Choice<br>Moderate | | | | | | |
| | | | | | | | |
| 11/1/2019 | Porky Pig<br>One Choice<br>Moderate | | | | | | |
| | | | | | | | |
| 12/1/2019 | Porky Pig<br>One Choice<br>Moderate | | | | | | |
| | | | | | | | |
| | | | | | | | |

# Designation of Beneficiary Form

| Designation of Beneficiary Form |
|---|
| In the event I die or Become Mentally Incapable of taking care of my Financial Affairs while I'm a member of the Financial Freedom Investment Club, I want all of my Shares to go to: _____ |
| If _____ Dies before me, I want all of my Shares to: go to: _____ <br><br> _____ <br> Member's Signature <br><br> _____ <br> Date of Signature |
| Beneficiary's Address: |
| Phone Number: |
| Second Beneficiary's Address: |
| Phone Number: |

# Chart to Save $100.08 in one Year

| Chart to Save $100.08 a Year By: John C. Jones | | | |
|---|---|---|---|
| Months | Amount | Formula | BAL |
| 1 | $8.34 | 8.34 X 1 | $8.34 |
| 2 | $8.34 | 8.34 X 2 | $16.68 |
| 3 | $8.34 | 8.34 X 3 | $25.02 |
| 4 | $8.34 | 8.34 X 4 | $33.36 |
| 5 | $8.34 | 8.34 X 5 | $41.70 |
| 6 | $8.34 | 8.34 X 6 | $50.04 |
| 7 | $8.34 | 8.34 X 7 | $58.38 |
| 8 | $8.34 | 8.34 X 8 | $66.72 |
| 9 | $8.34 | 8.34 X 9 | $75.06 |
| 10 | $8.34 | 8.34 X 10 | $83.40 |
| 11 | $8.34 | 8.34 X 11 | $91.74 |
| 12 | $8.34 | 8.34 X 12 | $100.08 |

# BASIC INVESTMENT TERMINOLOGY

**12B-1 Charge** - An added annual charge in a mutual fund that charges shareholders for some of the fund's promotion expenses.

**Adjusted Gross Income** _ Total income less allowed adjustments, which include such items as moving expenses, IRA, and Keogh contributions, and employee business expenses.

**ASK** - The lowest price a seller is willing to accept when selling a security (stock).

**Back-Ended Load Mutual Fund** - Additional charges and fees paid out annually rather than initially, unless money is withdrawn early, then a surrender charge or deferred sales charge takes effect.

**Balanced Fund** - A mutual fund that invests in both stocks and bonds.

**Bear Market** - A declining market, may refer to entire market or individual security.

**BID** - The highest price a buyer is willing to accept when purchasing a security (stock).

**Blue-Chip Stocks** - Shares of a large, mature company with a steady record of profits and dividends and a high probability of continued earnings.

**Bond** - A long term promissory note, prices go up when interest rates go down.

**BOOK VALUE** - The value of a company if all liabilities were subtracted from total assets.

**BROKER** - A person who buys or sells an investment for you in exchange for a fee called commission.

**Bull Market** - A rising market.

**Long Term Capital Gains** - The difference between an asset's purchase price and selling price, on holdings of more than twelve months.

**Capital Preservation** - Protecting the initial investment from loss of principal, typically accomplished by investing in conservative or guaranteed vehicles.

**Closed-End Mutual Fund** - Issues a limited number of shares and does not redeem those that are outstanding. Trades at a premium or discount to Net Asset to Value (NAV). a share price is determined by pressures of supply and demand.

**Cost Basis** - Original price of an asset, used in determining capital gains. It usually is the purchase price, but in the case of an inheritance it is the appraised value of the asset at the time of the donor's death.

**Club** - A group of persons for a common purpose.

**Dilution** - Issuing additional shares, thereby reducing proportional ownership of existing shareholders.

**Distribution** - Pay out of realized capital gains on securities in the portfolio of the fund or closed end investment company.

**Diversification** - Spreading of risk by putting assets in several categories of investments or with a broad range of stocks in one portfolio.

**Dividend** - A share of the company's net profits distributed by the company to its stockholders.

**Dollar Cost Averaging** - A formula-investment plan requiring periodic fixed-dollar-amount investments. This practice tends to average the unit cost of an investment over time.

**DOW JONES INDUSTRIAL AVERAGE (DJIA)** - It is the most popular and widely used measure of the U.S. Stock Market. It consists of a price-weighted list of 30 highly-traded Blue Chip Companies. The Dow is watched by investors as an indicator of the health and direction of the stock market.

**EARNINGS / PROFIT** - That portion of income left over after meeting all costs, overhead and taxes during a reporting period. This is called the Bottom Line. When a company is making money, it is said to be "in the black." When a company is losing money, it is "in the red."

**Embedded (OR Inherited) Unrealized Gains** - Unrealized gains within a mutual fund that would create a tax liability upon sale, even for new investors that did not participate in the gains.

**Emerging Markets** - Developing foreign markets, involving greater volatility and higher risk than established markets.

**Equities** - May be stock, bond, or options (securities).

**Growth** - Investments that will provide capital appreciation over the long-term.

**INCOME / REVENUE / SALES** - What a company earns for the goods they produce, or the services they provide. It is not the same as profit.

**Index Fund** - A fund whose portfolio is matched to an index, such as S&P, and whose performance therefore mirrors the market as a whole. (Usually have low fees and are tax efficient in bull markets).

**Inflation Protection** - Investing a portion of the portfolio in growth stocks or funds in order to keep up with the rise in the price of goods and services.

**Invest** - To buy in anticipation of future profit.

**Investment Club** - A group of persons for the common purpose of combining resources in the hope and anticipation of future profit.

**Junk Bond** - High Risk Bonds, usually promising a very high indicated return coupled with a larger risk of default.

**Load Fund** - Mutual Fund with shares sold at it's NAV plus a sales charge (typically 4-8%) of the net amount invested.

**Long Position** - The ownership of stocks or other securities, as opposed to a short position where one has sold securities that are not owned and want the price to go down.

**Low-Load Fund** - Mutual Fund that typically charge a 1-3% sales charge rather than a full load of 4-8%).

**MARKET CAPITILIZATION** - Also known as "market cap." It is calculated by multiplying the current price per share with the number of shares outstanding.

**Market Timing** - Market timing is the method of investing in certain asset classes at certain times to improve your returns – particularly stocks. Essentially, market timers try to outguess the trend of stocks or other prices. Although market timing may sound tempting, it has proven to be difficult to do well over the long-term. It may seem easy to wait for a market decline and then buy stocks before prices start going up, but much of the appreciation of stocks comes in brief, unexpected spurts that catch most investors off guard. Usually, by the time a new trend is evident, a significant portion of the appreciation has already passed.

**MONEY-MARKET ACCOUNT** - An interest bearing account where cash is held, generally a safer haven.

**MUTUAL FUND** - An open ended investment company that invests money of it's shareholders in a diversified group of securities of other corporations.

**NET ASSET VALUE (NAV)** – is value per share of a mutual fund or an exchange traded fund (ETF) on a specific date or time. With both security types, the pershare dollar amount of the fund is based on the total value of all the securities in its portfolio, any liabilities the fund has and the number of fund shares outstanding.

**NO-LOAD FUND** - A fund whose shares are bought and sold directly at the fund's NAV. Unlike a load fund, no agent or sales fee is involved, true no loads avoid deferred sales charges and 12b-1 fees.

**P / E RATIO** - How much money you are paying for $1 of the company's earnings. In other words, if a company reports a profit of $3 per share, and the stock is selling for $30 per share, the P/E Ratio is 10 because you are paying ten-times earnings ($30 per share divided by $3 per share earnings = 10 P/E.

**PENNY-STOCK** - Low priced stocks, usually considered under $1 per share, but sometimes includes stocks below $3.

**PORTFOLIO** - A holding of one or more securities by a single owner (institution or individual).

**PREFERRED STOCK** - Shares whose indicated dividends and liquidation values must be paid before common shareholders receive any dividends or liquidation payments.

**PROSPECTUS** - An official document that all companies offering new securities for public sale must file with the SEC.

**REDEMPTION** - Liquidating a shareholder's holdings.

**RISK** - The degree of uncertainty and chance of loss of principal regarding an investment.

**SECURITIES** - Paper assets representing a claim on something of value, such as stocks, bonds, mortgages, etc.

**SPLIT** - A securities transaction exchange whereby each shareholder ends up with more shares representing the same percentage of the firm. (Reverse split is when you get less shares).

**SPREAD** - The difference between Ask and Bid.

**STOCK** - Ownership shares in a corporation.

**TAX EFFICIENT FUNDS** - Funds that are managed to create a minimum tax situation, but be aware of embedded unrealized gains.

**TENDER OFFER** - An offer to purchase a large block of securities made outside the general market in which the securities are traded. Such offers are often made as part of an effort to take-over a company.

**TOTAL RATE OF RETURN** - An annual return on an investment including appreciation and dividends or interest.

**VOLATILITY** - Characteristics of a security, commodity, or market to rise or fall sharply in price within a short period of time, driven by emotions of fear and greed.

**VOLUME** - The number of shares of stock traded in a day.

**YIELD** - When a company pays a dividend, the yield is the percentage of dividend over the stock price. In other words, if a stock is trading for $10 and pays a dividend of $0.50, the yield is 5%, because for every $10 you invest, you would receive %% back annually being $0.50.

## THIS BOOK IS FOR THOSE WHO…

Desire to earn maximum profit on investments;

Desire clear and easy to understand information on group investing.

Desire to achieve financial security.

Realize there is the potential for greater profit with group investing.

Want to increase their readiness for retirement at an early age.

In conclusion, I am very confident that you are well on your way to enhancing your Financial Future with the start of an investment club.

Please e-mail me at john.jones6190@yahoo.com with questions, progress or comments. I look forward to hearing of your success on this journey and to learning how you built your "Financial Empire."

# ABOUT THE AUTHOR

John C. Jones is a person who just got tired of the traditional way of thinking (working on a job for 40 years and getting a gold watch, if you're lucky). That's why he developed this easy to follow Investment Guide for anyone who wants to plan their own Financial Future and Retirement.

He earned a B. S. Degree in Sociology from Tuskegee University, with a Minor in Psychology.

He earned his MBA from American Intercontinental University on July 22, 2017.

He started his very own Successful Investment Club on February 20, 1999. The club is still successful today. The club now has one Mutual Funds (this fund has twenty funds within it).

www.ingramcontent.com/pod-product-compliance
Lightning Source LLC
Chambersburg PA
CBHW020433220526
45464CB00002B/685